NICARAGUA

WESTVIEW PROFILES · NATIONS OF CONTEMPORARY LATIN AMERICA
Ronald Schneider, Series Editor

Guatemala: A Nation in Turmoil, Peter Calvert

†*Mexico: Paradoxes of Stability and Change,*
Daniel Levy and Gabriel Székely

†*Nicaragua: The Land of Sandino,* Second Edition,
Revised and Updated, Thomas W. Walker

†*The Dominican Republic: A Caribbean Crucible,*
Howard J. Wiarda and Michael J. Kryzanek

Colombia: Portrait of Unity and Diversity, Harvey F. Kline

Honduras: Caudillo Politics and Military Rulers, James A. Morris

†*Cuba: Dilemmas of a Revolution,* Juan M. del Aguila

Belize: A New Nation in Central America, O. Nigel Bolland

Bolivia: Land of Struggle, Waltraud Queiser Morales

Puerto Rico, Pamela S. Falk

Also of Interest

†*Latin American Politics and Development,*
Second Edition, Revised and Updated,
edited by Howard J. Wiarda and Harvey F. Kline

†*Latin America: Capitalist and Socialist Perspectives of Development
and Underdevelopment,* Ronald H. Chilcote and Joel C. Edelstein

†*Cuba's International Relations: The Anatomy of a Nationalistic Foreign
Policy,* H. Michael Erisman

†*Between Struggle and Hope: The Nicaraguan Literacy Crusade,*
Valerie Miller

†*The Fitful Republic: Economy, Society, and Politics in Argentina,*
Juan E. Corradi

†Available in hardcover and paperback.

ABOUT THE BOOK AND AUTHOR

From reviews of the first edition:

"*Nicaragua* is an excellent short introduction to a country of considerable contemporary relevance written by one of those most knowledgeable about it."

—Perspectives

"Walker is one of few American political scientists who did systematic research on Nicaragua before the revolution. The book is brief, elegantly written, and conveys invaluable information to novices as well as specialists. . . . The timeliness, high quality of design, presentation, and scholarship, plus the valuable pictures and annotated bibliography, all suggest that *Nicaragua: The Land of Sandino* will become a standard in courses on Latin America for years to come."

—Hispanic American Historical Review

"Walker's work . . . is valuable for the clarity of its presentation, the objectivity of its analysis, and the breadth of its coverage. The author presents an excellent summary of the political events leading up to the recent revolution."

—Library Journal

Drawing on numerous first-hand visits to Nicaragua since the Sandinist victory in 1979, Professor Walker has thoroughly updated his highly acclaimed book to reflect events in the new Nicaragua since the book's original publication in 1981. This second edition includes new material and photos in addition to an extensively updated bibliography.

Thomas W. Walker, an associate professor of political science at Ohio University, is the author of *The Christian Democratic Movement in Nicaragua* (1970). He is coauthor (with John A. Booth) of *Understanding Central America* (Westview, forthcoming) and editor of and contributor to *Nicaragua in Revolution* (1982), *Nicaragua: The First Five Years* (1985), and *Reagan vs. the Sandinistas: The Undeclared War on Nicaragua* (Westview, forthcoming). In 1982 he participated in the United Presbyterian Church's National Task Force on Central America and in 1983–1984 served as founding cochair of the Latin American Studies Association's National Task Force on Scholarly Relations with Nicaragua.

NICARAGUA

The Land of Sandino

SECOND EDITION, REVISED AND UPDATED

Thomas W. Walker

Westview Press / Boulder and London

Westview Profiles/Nations of Contemporary Latin America

The picture on the paperback cover, entitled *Amanecer en Nicaragua* (Awakening in Nicaragua), was drawn especially for this book by Leoncio Sáenz of Managua. An artist of considerable acclaim in Central America, Sáenz is a frequent artistic contributor to *Nicaráuac*, a monthly publication of the Nicaraguan Ministry of Culture.

Published in 1986 in the United States of America by Westview Press, Inc.; Frederick A. Praeger, Publisher; 5500 Central Avenue, Boulder, Colorado 80301

Library of Congress Cataloging-in-Publication Data
Walker, Thomas W.
    Nicaragua, the land of Sandino.
    (Westview profiles. Nations of contemporary Latin America)
    Bibliography: p.
    Includes index.
    1. Nicaragua—History. I. Title. II. Series.
F1526.W175 1986   972'.85   85-22566
ISBN 0-8133-0072-X
ISBN 0-8133-0073-8 (pbk.)

Printed and bound in the United States of America

10   9   8   7   6   5   4   3   2   1

To the Proud and Indomitable People of Nicaragua,
with Profound Respect and Love

Contents

List of Illustrations xi
Foreword, *Ronald Schneider*. xiii
Acknowledgments xv
Abbreviations xvii

1 Introduction 1

    Notes 7

**2 Early History: The Pre-Columbian Period
    to the Mid-1930s** 9

    The Pre-Columbian Period 9
    The Colonial Period: 1522–1822 10
    Independence 12
    The Walker Affair 13
    The Conservative Period: 1857–1893 15
    Zelaya and Zeledón 15
    The U.S. Occupation, the National Guard,
        and Sandino 19
    Notes 23

**3 Recent History: The Somoza Era and the
    Sandinist Revolution** 25

    The Rise of Anastasio Somoza García: 1933–1937 25
    The Rule of Anastasio Somoza García: 1937–1956 27
    Luis Somoza and the Puppets: 1957–1967 29
    Anastasio Somoza Debayle's First Term: 1967–1972 30
    The Beginning of the End: 1972–1977 31

The War of Liberation: 1978–1979 34
The Confluence of Grassroots Movements 40
The New Revolutionary Order......................... 42
Notes 52

4   *The Economic Dimension* 55

Evolution of the Economic System..................... 56
Sandinist Economic Policy............................. 66
Notes 73

5   *Culture and Society*................................... 75

Culture.. 75
Society 79
Revolutionary Social Programs 88
Notes 97

6   *Government and Politics* 99

The Prerevolutionary System.......................... 99
The Government of National Reconstruction............ 104
Groups and Power 107
The 1984 Elections and the New Governmental
    System 116
Notes 120

7   *The International Dimension*......................... 123

Nicaragua as a Client State 123
Revolutionary Nicaragua 131
Notes 141

Sources in English 145
    Books 145
    Periodicals... 155
Index 157

Illustrations

Map of Nicaragua.. xx
Some Nicaraguans
  Ranchhand 4
  Mother and child 4
  Boys with slingshot 5
  Market woman... 5
A sinister embrace: Anastasio Somoza García and
  Augusto C. Sandino..................................... 26
Fighting at the barricades.................................... 39
The Triumph—July 19, 1979 40
A Sandinista militiawoman and friends 50
The 1981 cotton harvest
  Volunteer labor: Urban workers 70
  Volunteer from the Sandinist Popular Army 70
Ruined grain storage facility................................. 71
Cartoon commentary on the attitude of the
  privileged classes....................................... 87
The 1980 Literacy Crusade
  Volunteer teachers depart for rural areas 94
  Teaching at night in unlikely locations................... 94
  Celebration in August 95
  Follow-up education for the newly literate................. 95
Whispering greed: Anastasio Somoza Debayle and
  Luis Manuel Debayle.................................... 103
The FSLN Directorate 105
Grassroots mobilization
  Liberation theologist Teófilo Cabestrero
  takes notes 108
  Leaders of UNAG conduct a meeting..................... 108
Members of the rebel militias 110

A seventeen-year-old veteran and a friend 111
Posters and murals
    A mural depicts the popular insurrection.................. 112
    A billboard states "Today the new dawn ceased
        to be an illusion" 112
    A billboard stresses the virtues of breast feeding 113
Nicaragua under siege
    Nicaraguans in the militia 138
    A member of a self-defense agricultural community......... 138
    Urban dwellers in a trench 139
    A segment of the U.S. community in Managua 139

Foreword

For many countries of Latin America, as well as for much of the rest of the so-called Third World, dependency is a basic fact of life. Related to, yet differentiated from, the elemental Marxist concept of imperialism, dependency theory in recent years has evolved into a framework for analyzing the political dilemmas and developmental processes of such countries. It has proved most useful when applied to frustrated or even abortive experiences with modernization, especially those cases in which the most intractable problems are rooted in a peripheral relationship to the international economic system and subordination to one of the world's superpowers in the political realm. As this has been the fundamental situation of Nicaragua until very recently, a modified dependency perspective is highly appropriate for Professor Walker's insightful study of this troubled Central American nation.

Nicaragua, with its long history of dictatorships and foreign intervention, followed by a dramatic revolution at the end of the 1970s, is certainly a most timely choice for the first volume in the *Nations of Contemporary Latin America* series. Here the United States, once it replaced Great Britain as the Western Hemisphere paramount (around the turn of the century), exercised an all but suffocating influence—one which produced both the Somoza dynasty and the Sandinist revolutionaries. Significantly, the confrontation between the original protagonists in this prolonged drama, Augusto César Sandino and Anastasio Somoza García, occurred during the early years of Franklin D. Roosevelt's Good Neighbor Policy when the United States was beginning to pull back from its most heavy-handed direct domination of Latin America. It would take nearly a half century for the political heirs of the martyred Sandino to topple the *Somocista* system erected during the 1930s, and great questions concerning the essential nature of the postrevolutionary regime remain to be resolved in the 1980s.

This book, like its sister studies in the series that will employ other analytical approaches to countries whose essential problems are of a significantly different nature, does not attempt to predict the future course of events. Its author does, however, meet the challenge of presenting a coherent interpretation of Nicaraguan reality, which will make controversial events intelligible to those seeking answers along the way to the questions of why developments are following a certain course. This is a critical contribution at a point in time when the Reagan administration in Washington appears strongly inclined to reassert the traditional U.S. voice and presence in the post-Somoza processes. Developments in and concerning Nicaragua during the late 1980s are giving rise to heated debate. This perceptive profile should provide needed focus and understanding to this debate and assure that at least some of the participants are well informed on the serious issues involved.

Ronald Schneider

Acknowledgments

I would like to express my gratitude to a number of individuals, groups, and institutions who helped produce this book. First, thanks are due the Nicaraguan people and government for their kind hospitality and extensive cooperation. I am also indebted to the Department of Political Science, the College of Arts and Sciences, and the Office of Research and Sponsored Programs at Ohio University for the financial support that enabled me to make numerous trips to Nicaragua following the liberation. For kindly agreeing to read and comment on various segments of the manuscript, thanks are due Alejandro Bendaña, Ricardo Chavarría, Joseph Collins, Kenneth P. Erickson, Peter Kemmerle, Susan E. Ramírez-Horton, Charles Roberts, Charles Stansifer, Eric Wagner, Anne U. Walker, and Sergio Zeledón. I am also grateful to the editors of *Caribbean Review*, *Current History*, Houghton Mifflin and Company, and Scholarly Resources, Inc., for their kind permission to use occasional phrases, sentences, and paragraphs that appeared in earlier works of mine for which they hold the copyrights. The work of several efficient and dedicated typists is also gratefully acknowledged. Finally, my deep appreciation goes to my wife, Anne, and my children, Joe, Carlos, Jimmy, and Emilie, for understanding and support beyond the call of duty.

T.W.W.

Abbreviations

AMNLAE	Luisa Amanda Espinosa Association of Nicaraguan Women
AMPRONAC	Association of Women Confronting the National Problem
ANS	Sandinist Children's Association
ASTC	Sandinist Association of Cultural Workers
ATC	Rural Workers' Association
CDC	Civil Defense Committee
CDRS	Ramiro Sacasa Democratic Coordinating Committee
CDS	Sandinist Defense Committee
CEB	Christian Base Community
CONDECA	Central American Defense Council
COPPPAL	Permanent Conference of Political Parties of Latin America
COSEP	Superior Council of Private Enterprise
CST	Sandinist Workers' Central
CTN	Social Christian Confederation of Workers of Nicaragua
CUS	Confederation of Labor Unity
DN	Sandinista Directorate
ENABAS	National Foodstuffs Enterprise
EPS	Sandinist Popular Army
FAO	Broad Opposition Front
FIR	International Reconstruction Fund (Nicaragua)
FPR	Revolutionary Patriotic Front
FSLN	Sandinist Front of National Liberation
GPP	Prolonged Popular War (faction)
IDB	Inter-American Development Bank
INCAE	Central American Institute of Business Administration

INPRHU	Institute of Human Promotion
INSSBI	Nicaraguan Social Security and Welfare Institute
JGRN	Governing Junta of National Reconstruction
JMRs	Municipal Juntas for Reconstruction
JS-19	19th of July Sandinist Youth
MAP-ML	Marxist Leninist Popular Action Movement
MDN	Nicaraguan Democratic Movement
MINVAH	Ministry of Housing and Human Settlements
MPS	Sandinist Popular Militias
OAS	Organization of American States
PCD	Democratic Conservative party
PCN	Nicaraguan Communist party
PLC	Constitutional Liberal party
PLI	Independent Liberal party
PPSC	Popular Social Christian party
PRI	Institutional Revolutionary party (Mexico)
PS	Sandinist Police
PSCN	Nicaraguan Social Christian party
PSD	Social Democratic party
PSN	Nicaraguan Socialist party
SI	Socialist International
SSTV	Sandinista Television System
TP	Proletarian Tendency
TPAs	Popular Anti-*Somocista* Tribunals
UNAG	National Union of (Small) Farmers and Cattlemen
UPANIC	Union of Nicaraguan Farmers

NICARAGUA

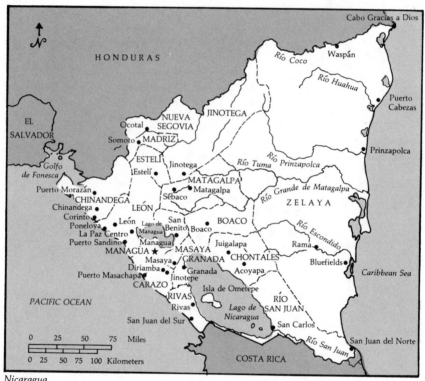

Nicaragua

1

Introduction

Located at the geographic center of Central America, with Honduras to the north and Costa Rica to the south, Nicaragua is the largest country in the region. Even so, its 57,143 square miles (148,000 square kilometers) of surface make it only slightly larger than the state of Iowa. Its population of about 3 million is slightly larger than Iowa's 2.8 million. Nevertheless, Nicaragua is an extremely interesting and unique country with an importance that far exceeds its size. Although there have been many revolts and coups d'etat in Latin America, Nicaragua is one of only a handful of Latin American countries to have experienced a real social revolution, by which I mean a rapid process of change in social and economic as well as political structures.

The physical characteristics of Nicaragua have long drawn the attention and captured the imagination of outsiders. The country has abundant and rich agricultural lands, considerable potential for geothermal and hydroelectric energy, important timber and mineral resources, and conveniently located waterways that make Nicaragua an ideal site for an interoceanic canal.

Though located entirely within the tropics, this small country varies from one region to another in temperature and other climatic characteristics. Altitude, mountainous land barriers, and the differing meteorological influences of the Caribbean and Pacific Ocean are the determining factors. As throughout the tropics, altitude rather than season determines temperature. On the lowlands of the Pacific and Caribbean coasts temperatures usually are quite high. In the central mountain ranges—or Cordilleras—that transverse the country from northwest to southeast, the climate is temperate. The mountains also influence Nicaraguan weather by acting as a natural barrier between the predominantly humid environment of the Caribbean and the seasonally dry patterns of the Pacific.

As a result of these factors, Nicaragua can be divided conceptually into three distinct regions: the Caribbean lowlands, the central highlands, and the western lowlands. Occupying nearly half of the country, the Caribbean lowlands are composed of hot, humid, tropical rain forests, swamps, and savannahs. As the most appropriate type of agricultural activity in such an environment involves the primitive technique of slash-and-burn, this vast region has never been able to support a large human population—at present less than 8 percent of the national total lives there.

Due to the more moderate and seasonal nature of rainfall in the central highlands and western lowlands, these regions are more inviting for commercial agriculture and human habitation. The temperate climate and rich soils of the highlands make an ideal environment for coffee cultivation. Indeed, some of the best coffee in the world comes from the highland department of Matagalpa. The western lowlands are appropriate for such crops as cotton, rice, and sugar. A chain of volcanos running through the western lowlands from northwest to southeast enriches the soil of the region through frequent dustings of volcanic ash. The principal cities and most of the population of Nicaragua are in the western lowlands.

Another important physical factor is the position of certain large lakes and rivers. Even in the colonial period, explorers and settlers knew that interoceanic travel across Nicaragua was possible via water routes, taking advantage of the San Juan River, Lake Nicaragua, and Lake Managua. The amount of overland travel required to complete the journey was small. As a result Nicaraguan waterways were regularly used as commercial routes for transisthmian travel during the nearly three centuries of colonial rule. And, in the nineteenth and twentieth centuries, the country's obvious potential as a canal site made Nicaragua the object of frequent foreign intrigue and intervention.

Nicaragua is blessed not only in natural resources and environment but also in certain demographic, social, and cultural characteristics. First, unlike some Latin American countries, it is not overpopulated. Indeed, although it has an abundance of arable land, Nicaragua's population is relatively small. Second, the people are relatively homogeneous and culturally integrated. There are no major racial, ethnic, linguistic, or religious divisions. Practically all Nicaraguans are Catholic, speak Spanish, and share a common cultural heritage. The majority are mestizo, a mixture of Spanish and Indian. And, though there are some "pure" whites, Indians, and blacks, little racial prejudice exists. Finally, Nicaraguans are a congenial, outgoing people with every reason to be proud of things *nica*, such as their distinctive cookery, music, dialect, literary heritage, and sense of humor.

Ironically, in spite of its human and natural potential, Nicaragua is a poor country and the majority of the people have endured great oppression throughout history. Even in the late 1970s the annual gross national product (GNP) per capita was only a little over $800 (U.S.). And this statistic obscures the fact that income in Nicaragua was so unevenly distributed that 50 percent of the people probably had an annual disposable income of only $200. This, in turn, means that the average citizen lived in inadequate housing, ate poorly, and, prior to the 1979 revolution, had little access to education, health care, or other public services. In 1979 the estimated life expectancy at birth for the average Nicaraguan was fifty-three years—ten years less than the average for Central America and eighteen years less than the average for the Latin American nation with the greatest longevity, Cuba.[1]

The roots of Nicaragua's problem lie in a phenomenon that many social scientists refer to as *dependency*. Most countries in the world are dependent to one degree or another on other countries. Interdependence does not necessarily imply dependency. Dependency refers to a specific situation in which the economy of a weak country is externally oriented and the government is controlled by national and/or international elites or classes that benefit from this economic relationship. Whereas the dominant elites in an industrial country usually have an interest in maintaining a healthy society and, therefore, a citizenry capable of consuming at high levels, the rulers of a dependent society have no such interest because their markets are largely external. For them, the common citizen is important not as a potential consumer but rather as a source of cheap and easily exploitable labor. In such societies the means of production and income tend increasingly to be concentrated in a few hands. Though impressive growth in the GNP often occurs, significant benefits almost never "trickle down" to the people, no matter how long the process goes on and no matter how much development takes place.[2]

Prerevolutionary Nicaragua was an extreme case of this common phenomenon. Since the days of the Spanish conquest in the sixteenth century, the Nicaraguan economy had always been externally oriented and the people who exercised power had been the beneficiaries of this relationship. First, hundreds of thousands of Indians were exported as slaves. Later, when that "resource" was used up, the elites exported timber, beef, and hides. During the late nineteenth century, coffee became an important product on the world market. In the twentieth century, especially after the Second World War, the country developed

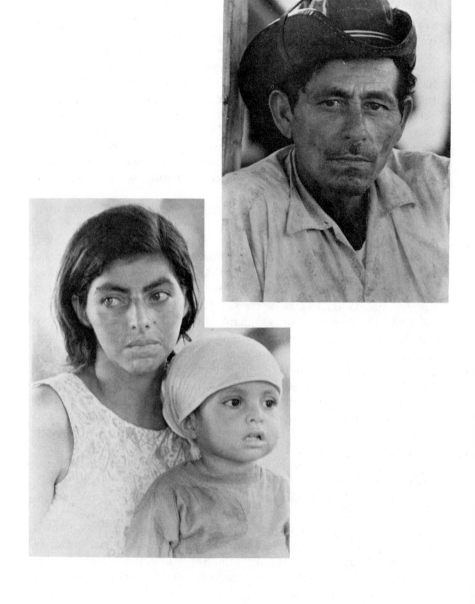

Some Nicaraguans. *Upper left,* ranchhand; *lower left,* mother and child (photos courtesy of Harvey Williams). *Upper right,* boys with slingshot; *lower right,* market woman (photos courtesy of Alberto Mendez of the Center for Agrarian Education and Promotion, Managua).

a diversified repertoire of exports ranging from cotton, coffee, and sugar to beef and gold. Throughout Nicaraguan history, a small elite controlled most of the means of production and garnered most of the benefits. The country's rulers—whether openly dictatorial or ostensibly democratic—always governed in behalf of the privileged few.

Paralleling this history of domestic exploitation—and frequently an essential ingredient of it—was a history of foreign intervention and control. During the colonial period, the Spanish faced sporadic challenges from the British government and English pirates for control of Nicaraguan territory. In the middle of the nineteenth century, the country was actually ruled by a U.S. citizen for a brief period. In the twentieth century, the U.S. government imposed its dominion over Nicaragua first by direct armed intervention (from 1912 to 1925 and from 1926 to 1933) and later through the client dictatorships of the Somoza family (from 1936 to 1979).

Yet if dependency, exploitation, and mass deprivation constitute recurrent themes in Nicaraguan history, so, too, do the ideas of nationalism and popular resistance. Nicaraguan history and folklore are replete with nationalist heroes and martyrs: the Indian *cacique* ("chief"), Diriangén, who fought against the Spanish at the outset of the colonial period; Andrés Castro, who took a stand against the forces of the North American filibuster-president, William Walker, in the mid-nineteenth century; the liberal dictator José Santos Zelaya, who defied British and U.S. imperial designs at the turn of the century; Benjamín Zeledón and Augusto César Sandino, who fought the U.S. occupiers in the early twentieth century; and Carlos Fonseca Amador, a cofounder of the Sandinist Front of National Liberation (FSLN), who died in the guerrilla struggle against the Somoza dictatorship in 1976.

By their actions, these men preserved and reinforced in the Nicaraguan people a stubborn strain of irrepressibility and national pride. Finally, catalyzed into action early in 1978 by the brutal assassination of a prominent and beloved opposition newspaper editor, Nicaraguans of all classes rose up against the dictatorship of Anastasio Somoza Debayle and the system he represented. Eighteen months later, at a cost of approximately fifty thousand dead, the Nicaraguan revolution had triumphed. A brutal and selfish dictator had been overthrown, and a revolutionary government representing the aspirations of countless generations of Nicaraguans had finally come to power.

The Nicaraguan people were aware of the historic significance of their victory. In spite of the tremendous cost of the war, the mood in the country in July 1979 was one of near universal ecstasy. On July 20, the largest crowd ever assembled in Central America greeted the new government in the central plaza. As one young woman said a few days later, after detailing the loss of various family members, "That [the death and destruction] doesn't matter. The revolution triumphed! I feel as if I had just been born! Like a little baby with a whole life ahead of me!"

In a sense the people of Nicaragua *had* just been born. Almost immediately the new government took steps to reverse the centuries-old patterns of elite control and dominance. A substantial segment of the economy was nationalized, exports were put under strict government control, a massive literacy campaign was launched, and new ideas in health, housing, and public education were generated and put into practice. Though Nicaragua would continue to be dependent on exports, the old cycle of *dependency*, with all its human costs, would, it was hoped, be broken.

This book deals with the history of the Nicaraguan people and their social, economic, and political reality, past and present. It also examines the programs and policies—domestic and foreign—of the revolutionary government. The themes of elite exploitation, foreign manipulation, national resistance, and revolutionary redirection receive special attention. I hope this approach will help the reader not only to appreciate why the Nicaraguan revolution took place but also to understand the motivations behind the various programs that the revolutionary government began to carry out.

NOTES

1. *1979 World Population Data Sheet* (Washington, D.C.: The Population Reference Bureau, 1979).

2. For a good discussion of *dependency*, see Ronald H. Chilcote and Joel C. Edelstein, "Alternative Perspectives of Development and Underdevelopment in Latin America," in their edited work, *Latin America: The Struggle with Dependency and Beyond* (New York: John Wiley and Sons, 1974), pp. 1–87.

2

Early History: The Pre-Columbian Period to the Mid-1930s

The history of Nicaragua is among the most turbulent and interesting in all of the Americas. If, on the one hand, it features incredible elite exploitation, mass suffering, and foreign interference, it also includes a significant element of popular resistance, national pride, and human nobility.

THE PRE-COLUMBIAN PERIOD

Even before the arrival of the Spaniards in the sixteenth century, the territory that we now call Nicaragua apparently was not a land of human tranquility. A demographic outpost of various Meso- and South American Indian groups, Nicaragua was an ethnically complex region. The most obvious dissimilarities were between the various indigenous tribes of South American origin that lived in the rain forests and savannahs to the east of the Central Cordillera and the Meso-American groups that inhabited the more hospitable western regions. The former, though primarily hunters and gatherers, also engaged in slash-and-burn agriculture, as do some of their descendants today. The more culturally sophisticated inhabitants of the western regions, on the other hand, were sedentary agriculturalists who raised corn, beans, and vegetables and lived in established towns with populations sometimes numbering in the tens of thousands. The western tribes spoke a variety of Meso-American languages reflecting several distinct waves of settlement from what is today Mexico and northern Central America. Though the western Indians rarely had anything to do with their more primitive counterparts across the

9

mountains, contact and conflict among the tribes of the west were common. Warfare, slavery, and involuntary tribute by the weak to the strong were among the basic ingredients of pre-Columbian life in the west. In a sense, then, many of the traits that characterized colonial rule existed long before the first *conquistadores* set foot in the land.

THE COLONIAL PERIOD: 1522–1822

The Spanish conquest of Nicaragua was an extension of the colonization of Panama, which began in 1508. Plagued by internal conflict, disease, and Panama's inhospitable natural environment, the Spaniards were not in a position to expand their control to the immediate north for well over a decade. It was only in 1522 that Gil González, commanding a small band of explorers under contract to the Spanish crown, finally set foot in Nicaragua. The purpose of his expedition—like that of other *conquistadores*—was to convert souls and to obtain gold and other riches from the native population. Considering that he managed to convert close to thirty thousand Indians, carry off nearly ninety thousand pesos worth of gold, and discover what appeared to be a water link between the Caribbean and the Pacific, González's venture into Nicaragua was a clear success.

It was not without its anxious moments, however. Though at first submissive, some Indians eventually decided to resist the bearded strangers. One of these was the legendary chief, Diriangén, from the region around what is today Granada. Several days after an initial meeting with González, in which he promised to bring his people to the Spaniard for conversion, Diriangén returned to attack the outsiders with several thousand warriors, causing them to retreat overland to the Pacific Ocean. To make matters worse, before they reached the safety of their Pacific fleet, González and his men were also set upon by warriors under the command of another chief, Nicarao. It was 1524 before the Spanish, under Francisco Hernández de Córdoba, returned to Nicaragua and imposed their control over the region.

The early years of the colonial period had a profound and lasting impact on the nature of Nicaraguan society and politics. The most important and tragic result of the conquest was demographic—the near total destruction of the large Indian population of the region. Incredible as it seems, it appears that Spanish chroniclers and early historians may have been fairly accurate when they reported that an original native population of around a million was reduced to tens of thousands within a few decades of the arrival of Gil González.[1]

This incredible depopulation was the result of several factors. The outright killing of natives in battle, probably accounting for the demise of a few thousand, was the least significant factor. Death by exposure to diseases brought to the New World by the Spaniards was much more important. The fact that Indians had little natural immunity to such common ailments as measles and influenza resulted in an immediate and dramatic reduction in their numbers throughout the Americas. It is likely that hundreds of thousands of Nicaraguan Indians perished of disease within a few decades.

Slavery was a third important factor that reduced Nicaragua's native population. Claims by writers of those times that four to five hundred thousand natives were gathered and exported into bondage during the first two decades of the colonial period seem to stand up to close scholarly investigation. The archives of the times show that there were enough slave ships of sufficient capacity making frequent enough trips to have accomplished this exportation.[2] The demand for slaves throughout the Spanish colonies—and especially in Peru in the 1530s—was very high. Though the Spanish themselves captured some slaves, many more were turned over to them by "friendly" Indian chiefs as a form of obligatory tribute. The life expectancy of these unfortunate souls was short. Many—sometimes 50 percent or more—died during the sea journey from Nicaragua to their intended destination. Most of the rest perished in slavery within a few years. As a result, supply never caught up with demand and, although the Spanish crown tried unsuccessfully to stop this lucrative trafficking in human life, the slave boom came to an end only when the resource was all but depleted. By the 1540s the Indian population of western Nicaragua appears to have plummeted to between thirty and forty thousand—and it declined gradually for several decades thereafter.

The result of this demographic holocaust is that Nicaragua today, instead of being a predominantly Indian country, is essentially mestizo in racial type and almost exclusively Spanish in language and other aspects of culture. Though most of the cities and towns of the country bear Indian names reflecting the culture of their founders, few of the people who walk their streets today are aware of what the names mean or who the original inhabitants were.

Another legacy of the colonial period—this one primarily political—was the rivalry between the principal cities of León, to the northeast of Lake Managua, and Granada, on the northern shore of Lake Nicaragua. Though both were founded by Francisco Hernández de Córdoba in 1524, they differed from each other in important cultural, social, and economic characteristics. As it was originally felt that Granada would be the political capital of the colony, the more "aristocratic" *conquistadores* chose to settle there. Spanish soldiers of lower rank and social status were packed off to León to defend the colony against incursions and claims by other Spanish adventurers from the north. As it turned out, however, León, not Granada, became the administrative center of the country, and Granada found itself forced to submit to the rule of a series of corrupt administrators based in what it considered a culturally inferior city. To make matters worse, there were significant differences in the economic interests of the two cities. The wealth of the self-styled aristocrats in Granada was based largely on cattle and on trade with the Caribbean via Lake Nicaragua and the San Juan River. Though cattle also were important in the region around León, many of the Leonese were also involved in such middle-class occupations as ship building, the procurement and sale of pine products, and government service. International trade in León was oriented almost entirely toward the Pacific. The Catholic church hierarchy, though stationed in the administrative center in León, sympathized with the aristocrats in Granada. Mutual jealousy and suspicion between the Leonese and Granadinos festered in a controlled form until independence allowed it to boil over into open warfare.

Curiously, the most flamboyant and prosperous years of the colonial period in Nicaragua were the first few decades, the time of the conquest and the slave trade. Once the Indian population had been depleted, the colony became an underpopulated backwater. Indeed, there was actually a severe manpower shortage, which forced some gold mines to close and caused landowners increasingly to switch from labor-intensive crop production to cattle raising. The economic foundation of this now underdeveloped colony was adequate to support the lifestyle of the landowning aristocrats in Granada and the merchants of León, but insufficient to provide for general prosperity.

To make matters worse, from the mid-seventeenth century on, the debilitated colony was frequently plagued by pirate attacks. As a result, trade via both the Caribbean and the Pacific was restricted and at times interrupted. By the mid-eighteenth century, the British, who were openly supportive of the pirates, became so bold as to occupy and fortify parts of the Caribbean coast. They maintained some claim over that region for well over a century.

INDEPENDENCE

The end of colonial rule in Central America simply added to the woes of the common Nicaraguan, for it meant the removal of the one external force that had kept the elites of León and Granada from sending their people into open warfare against each other. Mutual resentment between the two cities had flared up in 1811, a decade before the expulsion of the Spanish. When León, after first leading Granada into an insurrection against the crown, reversed its position and supported the royal authorities, it left the Granadinos in miserable isolation to receive the brunt of Spanish revenge. Nicaragua won its independence in stages: first as a part of the Mexican empire of Agustín de Iturbide in 1822, then as a member of the Central American Federation in 1823, and finally as an individual sovereign state in 1838. Throughout this period, the Leonese, who eventually came to call themselves Liberals, and the Granadinos, who championed the Conservative cause, squabbled and fought with each other over the control of their country. After 1838, the chaos and interregional warfare intensified. Presidents came and went as one group or the other imposed temporary control.

With Spain out of the way, other foreign powers began to interfere in Nicaraguan affairs, with the objective of dominating the interoceanic transit potential of the infant country. The British had long maintained a presence on the east coast. In the eighteenth century they had actually set up a form of protectorate over the Miskito Indians in that region. In the 1840s U.S. expansion to the Pacific coast of North America and the discovery of gold in California stimulated intense U.S. interest in Nicaragua as the site for an interoceanic transit route. Therefore, when the British moved to consolidate their control over the Miskito Coast by seizing the mouth of the San Juan River, the United States became alarmed and protested vigorously to the British. In 1850 the two countries attempted to diffuse the potential for conflict by signing the Clayton-Bulwer Treaty, in which both sides forswore any unilateral attempt to colonize Central America or to dominate any transisthmian transit route.

THE WALKER AFFAIR

The treaty, however, failed to bring peace to Nicaragua. By the mid-1850s the two emerging themes of Nicaraguan political life—foreign interference and interregional warfare—converged to produce an important turning point and one of the most bizarre episodes in Central American history: the Walker affair. In spite of the Clayton-Bulwer Treaty, the clearly conflicting interests of the British and the Americans in the area had kept tension between the two countries at a high level. Both countries frequently took sides in Nicaraguan domestic politics—the British tending to support the Conservatives, and the Americans to support the Liberals. Finally, in 1854, the

Liberals, who were at the time losing in a struggle to unseat the Conservatives, turned for help to a San Franciso–based soldier of fortune named William Walker.[3]

Though often depicted as a simple villain, Walker was an extremely interesting and complex individual. The son of a pioneer family from Tennessee, he was graduated from college and earned a medical degree while still in his teens. He then pursued a law degree, practiced that profession for a short while, turned to journalism, and finally became a soldier of fortune—all before he had reached his midthirties. In some senses he was an idealist. As a journalist he championed the cause of abolition and, like many people of that era, he was a firm believer in manifest destiny—the imperialist expansion of Yankee ideals, by force if necessary, beyond the boundaries of the United States.

In accordance with his pact with the Liberals, Walker sailed in June 1855 from California to Nicaragua with a small band of armed Californians. After some initial military setbacks he and his Liberal allies took Granada in October and set up a coalition government under a Conservative, Patricio Rivas. Almost from the start, the real power in the government was Walker himself, who rapidly began to implement a series of liberal developmentalist ideas that included the encouragement of foreign investment and the increased exploitation of Nicaraguan resources. In July 1856, Walker formally took over the presidency.

Initially Walker seems to have had at least the tacit support of the U.S. government. His entrance into the Nicaraguan civil war met with no serious resistance from Washington, which was quick to recognize the puppet government of Patricio Rivas. However, the British and the governments of the other Central American countries were appalled by this bald-faced Yankee attempt to create a U.S. outpost on the Central American isthmus. And many Nicaraguans of both parties became increasingly alarmed at the foreign takeover of their country. This was especially true in 1856 when Walker, the dictator-president, legalized slavery and declared English to be the official language. As a result, it was not long before the onset of a war in which Nicaraguans of both parties and, at one time or another, troops from all of the Central American republics (armed and backed financially by England, certain South American countries, and a variety of public and private interests in the United States) fought against the hated foreigners. In the spring of 1857, the U.S. government intervened to arrange a truce and to allow Walker to surrender and leave Nicaragua. (Walker returned to Central America in yet another filibustering attempt in 1860, but he was captured by the British and turned over to the Hondurans, who quickly tried him and put him before a firing squad.) So important is the war against Walker in Nicaraguan patriotic lore that the independence day that *nicas* celebrate on September 14 is a commemoration of a decisive battle at San Jacinto against Walker and his U.S. troops.

THE CONSERVATIVE PERIOD: 1857–1893

For more than three decades following the defeat of Walker, the country enjoyed relative peace and stability. True, several thousand Indians lost their lives in 1881 in the tragic War of the Comuneros— a rebellion aimed at halting the takeover of their ancestral lands by wealthy coffee growers. But the elites of Nicaragua were temporarily at peace during this period. As a result of their association with the U.S. filibuster, the Liberals had been discredited. The Conservatives, therefore, were able to rule, without interruption and with only sporadic and halfhearted resistance from their traditional adversaries, from 1857 to 1893. A new constitution was adopted in 1857. Thereafter "elected" Conservative presidents succeeded each other at regular four-year intervals, breaking the old tradition of *continuismo* (an individual's self-perpetuation in power). The country was also blessed in this period with a relative lull in foreign interference, which came as a result of the completion in 1855 of a transisthmian railroad in Panama that temporarily took the pressure off Nicaragua as a focal point of interoceanic transit. And finally, during these decades Managua, which had become the capital in 1852, grew and prospered as a result of a coffee boom in that area.

ZELAYA AND ZELEDÓN

Conservative rule, however, was not to last. In 1893 the Liberals, under the leadership of José Santos Zelaya, joined dissident Conservatives in ousting the Conservative government of Roberto Sacasa. Three months later they overthrew the dissident Conservative whom they had initially placed in power and replaced him with Zelaya himself. For the next sixteen years Zelaya was not only the dictator of Nicaragua but also one of the most important figures in Central American regional politics.

Zelaya was a controversial and unjustly maligned figure. He is commonly described in U.S. textbooks on Central and Latin American history as a corrupt, brutal, cruel, greedy, egocentric, warmongering tyrant. In 1909 President William Howard Taft denounced him as "a blot on the history of Nicaragua." Careful examination of the facts, however, reveals that this depiction has much less to do with the reality of Zelaya's rule than with official U.S. frustration and resentment over the Liberal dictator's stubborn defense of national and Central American interests in the face of burgeoning U.S. interference in the affairs of the region following the Spanish-American War.[4]

Zelaya would be described more accurately as a relatively benevolent, modernizing, authoritarian nationalist. Born in Managua in 1853, the son of a Liberal coffee planter, he was educated at the Instituto de Oriente in Granada. At sixteen he was sent to France for further studies, and there he became imbued with the positivist philosophies of Auguste Comte and Herbert Spencer. When he returned to his homeland at nineteen, he immediately entered politics. Subsequently, as the young mayor of Managua, he set up a lending library and stocked it with the works of the French philosophers.

There is no doubt that, as dictator of Nicaragua, Zelaya used whatever means necessary to keep himself in power. Democracy did not exist; freedom of the press was often curtailed. It is also true that Zelaya was certainly no great social reformer. But there is little evidence of his alleged cruelty. His constitution of 1893 abolished the death penalty and he apparently made a practice of granting amnesty, after a decent interval, to captured opposition insurgents.

What is more important, Zelaya initiated many reforms in Nicaragua. In the first place, he worked to secularize Nicaraguan society; his constitution separated church and state and guaranteed freedom of religion and free secular education, and he financed the opening of new schools and the training of Nicaraguans abroad. By the end of his rule, the government was devoting approximately 10 percent of the budget to education.

Like other Latin American positivist leaders of the time, he made a significant effort to modernize the economy. His government surveyed and opened new lands for the expansion of the coffee industry. It also fostered the collection and storage of information by setting up the National Archives and Museum, reorganizing the General Statistics Office, and conducting a national census. In addition, his government invested in the physical infrastructure of communication by purchasing steamships and building roads and telegraph lines. As a result of these modernizing efforts, there was, during the Zelaya period, a rapid increase in the production of such export commodities as coffee, bananas, timber, and gold.

In foreign affairs, Zelaya worked to defend Nicaraguan interests and to promote Central American reunification. More effective in the former than in the latter, he is best known for his success in getting the British to withdraw once and for all from the Miskito Coast. Although they had essentially agreed to withdraw in the 1860 Treaty of Managua, they had not done so. In 1894, Zelaya sent troops to the city of Bluefields, accepted the Miskito king's petition for incorporation, and expelled the protesting British consul from the territory. The British responded with a blockade of Nicaragua's Pacific port, but the United States—anxious to enforce the Monroe Doctrine—pressured them to back down and to accept full Nicaraguan sovereignty over the disputed area.

Zelaya's efforts at promoting Central American reunification, though unsuccessful, were significant. Capitalizing on a region-wide resurgence of Central American nationalism, stimulated in part by his own success in confronting the British on the Miskito Coast, Zelaya convened the Conference of Amapala in 1895, in which Nicaragua, Honduras, and El Salvador agreed to form a confederation called the *República Mayor* (the Greater Republic). A diplomatic representative was dispatched to the United States and received by President Grover Cleveland, and a constitution for this larger political entity was written in 1898. Unfortunately, before it could go into effect the incumbent government of El Salvador was overthrown and the new government withdrew from the union. The confederation subsequently collapsed.

Much is made in some accounts of the apparent fact that Zelaya was a disrupter of the peace in Central America. He did, indeed, invade neighboring Honduras on two occasions. However, it is equally true that he preferred to let the *República Mayor* collapse rather than send troops to El Salvador to hold it together by force. In addition, he settled boundary disputes with both of Nicaragua's neighbors through arbitration rather than by force. In the case of the boundary dispute with Honduras, he peacefully accepted a settlement that went against Nicaragua's claims.

Zelaya's downfall in 1909 was largely the result of a mounting conflict with the United States. It is important to remember that in that country at the turn of the century "imperialism" was not a dirty word. The Spanish-American War had given the United States a colonial empire and many Americans felt that their country had a legitimate colonial role to play in Central America. Zelaya's assertion as a regional leader and champion of Central American unity was, at least in part, a response to this threat—a response Washington resented. Zelaya also had the audacity to refuse to grant the United States canal-building rights that would have included U.S. sovereignty over certain Nicaraguan territory. As a result, the United States became involved in engineering Panamanian "independence" from

Colombia and in 1903 signed the treaty it wanted with the new government it had helped create. A few years later the Americans became alarmed with rumors that Zelaya was negotiating with the British and the Japanese to build a second—and potentially competitive—canal through Nicaragua.

The upshot of these and other sources of friction between the United States and Zelaya was that Washington eventually let it be known that it would look kindly on a Conservative overthrow of Zelaya. In 1909, when the revolt finally took place in Bluefields, Zelaya's forces made the tactical mistake of executing two confessed U.S. mercenaries. The United States used this incident as an excuse to sever diplomatic relations and to send troops to Bluefields to ensure against the defeat of the Conservatives. Though he held on for a few more months, Zelaya was ultimately forced to accept the inevitable, to resign, and to spend the rest of his life in exile.

Before his resignation, Zelaya attempted to save the situation for his party by appointing a highly respected Liberal from León, Dr. José Madriz, to succeed him. The U.S. government, however, was determined that the Zelayista Liberals relinquish control. Washington refused to recognize the new government and early in 1910, when Madriz's troops succeeded in routing the rebel forces in an attempted thrust to the west and drove them back to Bluefields, the commander of U.S. forces in that town forbade government troops from attacking rebel positions. In the face of such foreign interference, it was impossible for the Liberals to win, much less to govern. On August 20, 1910, the Madriz government collapsed and was replaced by a puppet, pro-U.S. regime supported by the Conservatives and some opportunistic Liberal *caudillos* (leaders).

For the next two years (1910–1912), the economic and political situation deteriorated rapidly. The rebellion had disrupted the planting of crops and disturbed other sectors of the economy and, although the Madriz government had left the national treasury with a favorable balance, the new government squandered this resource almost immediately and began wildly printing paper money. Washington arranged private bank loans to its new client regime, but much of the loan money went almost immediately into the pockets of corrupt politicians. It was necessary to renegotiate loans and to allow the United States to become involved in the supervision of customs collection and the management of payment of the foreign debt.

The abysmal situation into which the country had fallen offended the national pride of many Nicaraguans, among them a young Zelayista Liberal, Benjamín Zeledón. A teacher, newspaperman, and lawyer, Zeledón had served Zelaya's government as a district judge in the newly liberated Atlantic territories, as an officer in the war with

Honduras in 1907, as Nicaragua's representative to the Central American Court of Justice, and finally, at the age of thirty, as minister of defense. Under the Madriz government, he had continued as minister of defense and been elevated to the rank of general of the armies. In July 1912, when a group of dissident Conservatives rebelled against puppet president Adolfo Diaz, Zeledón and a group of Liberals joined in the uprising to rid Nicaragua of "the traitors to the Fatherland."

At first it appeared that the insurgents might win. Zeledón and his Liberal followers seized León and several other cities and cut communications to Managua. However, in the words of one U.S. observer of the times, "The U.S. could hardly permit the overthrow of the Conservative authorities. [If the rebels won] all of the efforts of the State Department to place Nicaragua on her feet politically and financially would have been useless, and the interests of the New York bankers . . . would be seriously imperiled."[5] Therefore, under the old pretext of protecting U.S. lives and property, U.S. Marines were sent into Nicaragua. Though resistance by dissident Conservatives was quickly overcome, Zeledón not only rejected U.S. demands that he, too, surrender but also warned the U.S. commander that he, his superiors, and the "powerful nation" to which he belonged would bear the "tremendous responsibility and eternal infamy that History will attribute to you for having employed your arms against the weak who have been struggling for the reconquest of the sacred rights of [their] Fatherland."[6]

Badly outnumbered by the combined U.S. and Nicaraguan government forces, Zeledón's troops were besieged and defeated, and he was captured by Nicaraguan troops. Though the United States was in a position to save Zeledón's life, Major Smedley D. Butler, in a telegram to his superiors, suggested that "through some inaction on our part someone might hang him."[7] Butler's advice was apparently taken, for, on the following day, the Conservative government announced that Zeledón had died in battle. Before the young patriot's body was buried, it was dragged through the little hamlet of Niquinohomo. There, by historical coincidence, a short, skinny, seventeen-year-old boy was among those who witnessed government troops kicking the lifeless form. This seemingly insignificant teenager—who later commented that the scene had made his "blood boil with rage"—was Augusto César Sandino.

THE U.S. OCCUPATION, THE NATIONAL GUARD, AND SANDINO

For most of the following two decades, Nicaragua was subjected to direct foreign military intervention. U.S. troops were stationed there from 1912 to 1925 and again from 1926 to 1933, an intervention apparently motivated by a variety of concerns. Relatively unimportant, though not negligible, was the desire to protect U.S. investment. The involvement of U.S. bankers in Nicaragua has been mentioned. There was also a sincere, if naive, belief in some circles that U.S. involvement could somehow help bring democracy to the country. The most important motivations, however, seem to have been geopolitical. U.S. decision makers felt it imperative to maintain a stable pro-U.S. government in Nicaragua, a country that, in addition to being an ideal site for a second transisthmian waterway, was located in the center of the U.S. sphere of influence in Central America.

During the first occupation, from 1912 to 1925, the United States ran Nicaraguan affairs through a series of Conservative presidents— Adolfo Diaz, Emiliano Chamorro, and Diego Manuel Chamorro. The relationship was symbiotic. The United States needed the Conservatives, and the Conservatives—who had neither the military strength nor the popular backing to maintain themselves in power—needed the United States. The Liberals were well aware that any attempt to regain power by means of an uprising would simply mean another unequal contest with the forces Zeledón faced in 1912, so an uneasy quiet prevailed.

The most notable product of the period was the Bryan-Chamorro Treaty, signed in 1914 and ratified in 1916. By the terms of this document the United States acquired exclusive rights, in perpetuity, to build a canal in Nicaragua, a renewable ninety-nine-year lease to the Great and Little Corn Islands in the Caribbean, and a renewable ninety-nine-year option to establish a naval base in the Gulf of Fonseca. In return, Nicaragua was to receive payment of three million dollars. In reality, however, the U.S. officials who ran Nicaraguan financial affairs channeled much of that paltry sum into payments to foreign creditors. The aspects of the treaty dealing with the Corn Islands and the Gulf of Fonseca were hotly contested by El Salvador and Costa Rica, and the Central American Court of Justice decided in their favor. Though the United States had originally played a principal role in the creation of the court, it now chose to ignore its decision and, in so doing, contributed significantly to its collapse a few years later.

By the mid-1920s, U.S. decision makers had convinced themselves that the Conservatives were ready to carry on without the presence of U.S. troops. They were wrong. Within a few months of the first U.S. withdrawal in August 1925, conflicts flared up among the ruling Conservatives and, in 1926, the Liberals seized the initiative and staged a rebellion. The inevitable outcome was that the Conservatives were forced to turn again to Washington for salvation and U.S. troops returned to Nicaragua.

During the second occupation Washington showed greater skill and imagination in manipulating Nicaraguan affairs. It arranged a truce between the Liberals and the Conservatives that, among other things, provided for a free U.S.-supervised election in 1928. Though José María Moncada, the candidate of the majority Liberal party, won that contest, the United States was prepared to live with a Liberal president for, in the words of one scholar, the North Americans "controlled his regime from a number of points: the American Embassy; the Marines . . . ; the Guardia Nacional, with its United States Army Officers; the High Commissioner of Customs; the Director of the Railway; and the National Bank."[8] Under the circumstances, it no longer mattered whether the chief executive was a Liberal or a Conservative. Increasingly secure in this fact, the Americans in 1932 oversaw yet another free election won by yet another Liberal—this time, Juan B. Sacasa, ironically the same person who had led the Liberal uprising of 1926 that brought about the second occupation.

The importance of this period (1927–1933) lies much less in the individuals who happened to occupy the presidency than in the fact that, during these six years, forces were being shaped that were to have a powerful and paradoxical impact on Nicaragua for at least the next half century. This was the time of the germination of the Somoza dictatorship, which was to rule Nicaragua for over four decades, and of the reinvigoration of a revolutionary nationalist tradition that would ultimately overthrow that dictatorship in favor of a radically new system.

The revolutionary tradition was dramatically resuscitated by Augusto César Sandino, who led a long guerrilla war against U.S. and government forces during the second occupation of his country. Sandino was a fascinating person. Born in 1895 of a common-law union between a moderately well-to-do landowner and an Indian woman, he was accepted by his father and nurtured philosophically in the high principles that were supposed to form the basis of Liberal practice. He worked for his father until he was twenty-five, when he fled Nicaragua after a fight in which he wounded a man who had insulted his mother. He eventually ended up in Tampico, Mexico, working for Standard Oil of Indiana. There he absorbed some of the ideals of the Mexican Revolution—in particular the emphasis on the dignity of the Indian. In 1926 he returned to Nicaragua and found employment in a U.S.-owned gold mine. When the Liberal insurrection broke out that year, he organized a fighting unit and joined the insurgents. In 1927, after the rest of the Liberals had agreed to the

U.S.-sponsored peace settlement, he chose to continue the battle against the puppet Conservative government. This decision inevitably brought him into conflict with U.S. troops and quickly turned his partisan crusade into a war of national liberation.

Though he wrote and spoke eloquently and profusely, Sandino was a man of action rather than a theorist. He did have certain ideas and opinions about the future of Nicaraguan politics and society. For instance, he advocated the formation of a popularly based political party and endorsed the idea of organizing land into peasant cooperatives. But more than anything else, he was a nationalist and an anti-imperialist. Quite simply, he found the U.S. occupation and domination of his country to be offensive and unacceptable. "The sovereignty and liberty of a people," he said, "are not to be discussed, but rather, defended with weapons in hand."[9]

In the struggle he led against U.S. and government troops, Sandino developed an effective set of guerrilla tactics through a process of trial and error. At first he used conventional military tactics, sending large groups of men into combat against an entrenched and well-equipped enemy. As a result, his troops initially took heavy casualties without inflicting serious damage. Learning from this mistake, he quickly developed the more classical guerrilla strategies of harassment and hit and run. In addition, he cultivated the support of the peasants in the regions in which he operated. They, in turn, served as an early warning communication network and as ad hoc soldiers during specific guerrilla actions.

The upshot of Sandino's activities was that the marines and government troops eventually found themselves bogged down in a costly Vietnam-type war that they simply could not win militarily. Practices such as the aerial bombardment of "hostile" towns and hamlets and the forced resettlement of peasant populations only intensified popular identification with the guerrilla cause. There were fluctuations in guerrilla activity and strength, but when the United States finally withdrew in January 1933, Sandino was still "as great a threat . . . as he had been at any previous point in his career."[10]

Ironically, the threat Sandino posed dissolved almost immediately after the Americans left. Because his major condition for peace had been the departure of the marines, Sandino signed a preliminary peace agreement, in February 1933, with the Sacasa government. Calling for a cessation of hostilities and a partial disarmament of the guerrillas, the document also guaranteed amnesty for Sandino's men and a degree of autonomy for those Sandinists who wished to settle in the territory along the Río Coco. In 1934 there were further peace negotiations. In the long run, however, Sandino was deceived, captured, and executed. But his daring stand against the foreign occupiers had been an example and had legitimized a set of tactics that were to be successfully employed by the Sandinist Front of National Liberation in overthrowing a U.S.-client dictatorship almost a half century later.

The other force that came into its own during the second U.S. occupation and had a profound impact on the future of the country was the National Guard of Nicaragua. Washington had long felt that what Nicaragua really needed was an apolitical constabulary that could maintain stability and create a healthy environment for political and economic development. Although a halfhearted attempt to create such a force had been made toward the end of the first occupation, the concept was not effectively implemented until the late 1920s. By then the United States was becoming increasingly tired of directly running Nicaragua's internal affairs. And, of course, there was the desire to "Nicaraguanize," if you will, the war against Sandino. Top priority, therefore, was placed on recruiting, training, arming, and equipping the *Guardia*. In the haste of the moment, safeguards aimed at maintaining the apolitical character of the guard were set aside. As the marines were leaving, command of this new "national" army passed from the Americans to a congenial, ambitious, English-speaking Nicaraguan politician, Anastasio Somoza García. Less than four years later, an elitist dictatorial system based on a symbiotic relationship between the now corrupted and thoroughly politicized National Guard and the Somoza family had come into being. This system was to plunder, degrade, and bring agony to the Nicaraguan people for more than four decades.

NOTES

1. For an excellent, scholarly examination of the early depopulation of Nicaragua, see David Richard Radell, "Native Depopulation and the Slave Trade: 1527–1578," in his *An Historical Geography of Western Nicaragua: The Spheres of Influence of León, Granada, and Managua, 1519–1965* (Ph.D. dissertation, University of California, Berkeley, 1969), pp. 66–80.

2. Ibid., pp. 70–80.

3. No known relation of the author of this volume.

4. For an excellent reexamination of Zelaya, see Charles L. Stansifer, "José Santos Zelaya: A New Look at Nicaragua's Liberal Dictator," *Revista/ Review Interamericana*, vol. 7, no. 3 (Fall 1977), pp. 468–485. The interpretation and much of the information in my short treatment of Zelaya is drawn from this fine source.

5. Dana G. Munro, *The Five Republics of Central America* (New York: Russell & Russell, 1967), p. 243.

6. A handwritten letter from Zeledón to Colonel J. H. Pendleton, Masaya, October 3, 1912. Xerox copy courtesy of Zeledón's grandson, Sergio Zeledón.

7. Major Smedley D. Butler as quoted in Richard Millett, *The Guardians of the Dynasty: A History of the U.S.-Created Guardia Nacional de Nicaragua and the Somoza Family* (Maryknoll, N.Y.: Orbis Books, 1977), p. 32.

8. Ralph Lee Woodward, Jr., *Central America: A Nation Divided* (New York: Oxford University Press, 1976), p. 200.

9. Though this is one of the best-known sayings from Sandino, we do not have the original citation.

10. Millett, *Guardians of the Dynasty,* p. 98.

3

Recent History:
The Somoza Era and
the Sandinist Revolution

In the Latin American context, Nicaraguan history since 1933 is unusual in at least two respects. First, though many other countries have suffered dictatorial rule, Nicaragua's forty-two-and-a-half-year subjugation to the Somozas was unique not only in its duration but also in its dynastic character. Nowhere else in Latin America has dictatorial power passed successively through the hands of three members of the same family. Second, Nicaragua is one of only a tiny handful of Latin American countries to have seriously attempted social revolution.

THE RISE OF ANASTASIO SOMOZA GARCÍA: 1933-1937

The founder of the Somoza dynasty, Anastasio Somoza García, was a complex and interesting individual. Born on February 1, 1898, the son of a moderately well-to-do coffee grower, "Tacho" Somoza was just short of thirty-five years when the departing marines turned over to him the command of the National Guard. His early ascent to this pivotal position of power was no mere accident. Intelligent, outgoing, persuasive, and ambitious, he was an unusual young man. He received his early education at the Instituto Nacional de Oriente and went on for a degree at the Pierce School of Business Administration in Philadelphia, where he perfected his English and met and married Salvadora Debayle, a member of one of Nicaragua's important aristocratic families. Upon his return to Nicaragua, he joined the Liberal revolt in 1926. Though he and his troops were ingloriously routed, he subsequently worked his way up in Liberal party politics,

25

eventually serving as minister of war and minister of foreign relations. A beguiling, gregarious young man with an excellent command of English, he got along well with the U.S. occupiers and was involved in the creation of the National Guard.

In the years immediately following the departure of the marines, Somoza worked efficiently to consolidate his control over the guard. In the wake of real or apparent anti-Somoza conspiracies, he purged various officers who might have stood in his way. Also, on February 21, 1934, he gave his subordinates permission to capture and murder Augusto César Sandino. In doing so, he not only eliminated a potential political rival but also endeared himself to many of the guardsmen, who harbored an intense hatred of the nationalist hero who had frustrated them for so long. Sandino's execution was followed by a mop-up operation in which hundreds of men, women, and children living in the semiautonomous region previously set aside for the former guerrillas were slaughtered. Finally, he encouraged guardsmen at all levels to engage in various forms of corruption and exploitative activities, thus isolating them from the people and making them increasingly dependent on their leader.

A sinister embrace: Anastasio Somoza García (left) and Augusto C. Sandino (right) a few days before Somoza's National Guard carried out the assassination of Sandino in 1934. (Photo courtesy of *Barricada*)

By 1936, Somoza was sufficiently sure of his control of the guard—and hence Nicaraguan politics—to overthrow the elected president, Juan B. Sacasa, and stage an "election" in which he was the inevitable winner. His inauguration on January 1, 1937, confirmed a fact that had long been apparent: In the wake of the U.S. occupation, the National Guard and its chief had become the real rulers of Nicaragua.

THE RULE OF ANASTASIO SOMOZA GARCÍA: 1937–1956

Somoza García was the dictator of Nicaragua for the next nineteen years. Occasionally, for the sake of appearance, he ruled through puppets, but for most of the period, he chose to occupy the presidency directly. In these years he developed an effective style of rule that was to characterize the Somoza dynasty until the late 1960s. The Somoza formula was really rather simple: maintain the support of the guard, cultivate the Americans, and co-opt important domestic power contenders.

The guard's loyalty was assured by keeping direct command in the family and by continuing the practice of psychologically isolating the guardsmen from the people by encouraging them to be corrupt and exploitative. Accordingly, gambling, prostitution, smuggling, and other forms of vice were run directly by guardsmen. In addition, citizens soon learned that in order to engage in any of a variety of activities—legal or not—it was necessary to pay bribes or kickbacks to guard officers or soldiers. In effect, rather than being a professional national police and military force, the guard was a sort of Mafia in uniform, which served simultaneously as the personal bodyguard of the Somoza family.

Somoza also proved to be very adept in manipulating the Americans. Though Washington did occasionally react negatively to his designs to perpetuate himself indefinitely in power, the beguiling dictator was always able in the end to mollify U.S. decision makers. In addition to personal charm, he relied heavily on political obsequiousness in maintaining U.S. support. His regime consistently backed U.S. foreign policy. Washington's enemies were automatically Somoza's enemies, be they the Axis powers in the late 1930s and early 1940s or the Communists thereafter. The United States was allowed to establish military bases in Nicaragua during the Second World War and to use the country as a training area for the CIA-organized counterrevolution against Guatemalan president Jacobo Arbenz in 1954. Somoza even offered to send guardsmen to fight in Korea. In return, Somoza was lavishly entertained at the White House and received lend-lease funds to modernize the National Guard.

The dictator was also clever in his handling of domestic power groups. After the murder of Sandino and his followers, he adopted a more relaxed policy toward the opposition. Human rights and basic freedoms—for the privileged at least—were more generally respected. Whenever possible, the Conservative leadership was bought off—the most notable example being the famous "pact of the generals" in which the Conservative chiefs agreed to put up a candidate to lose in the rigged election of 1951 in return for personal benefits and minority participation in the government.

In addition, Somoza pursued developmentalist economic policies that emphasized growth in exports and the creation of economic infrastructure and public agencies such as the Central Bank, the Institute of National Development, and the National Housing Institute. Although the unequally distributed growth produced by this developmentalism did not do much for the common citizen, it did benefit Somoza significantly. In addition to providing opportunities to expand his originally meager fortune to around $50 million (U.S.) by 1956, it also created vehicles for employing and rewarding the faithful.

The rule of Anastasio Somoza García came to an abrupt and unexpected end in 1956 as the dictator was campaigning for "election" to a fourth term as president. On September 20 a young poet named Rigoberto López Pérez infiltrated a reception honoring the dictator and pumped five bullets point-blank into Somoza's corpulent hulk. In a letter he had sent to his mother, with instructions that it be opened only in the event of his death, López explained, "What I have done is a duty that any Nicaraguan who truly loves his country should have done a long time ago."[1]

If López, who was immediately shot by Somoza's bodyguards, thought his *ajusticiamiento* (bringing to justice) of the dictator would rid his country of Somoza rule, he was sadly mistaken. Although he died a few days later (in spite of the very best emergency medical assistance the Eisenhower administration could provide), Somoza already had taken steps to assure a smooth transition of rule within his immediate family. His sons, Anastasio and Luis, had been educated in the United States, the former at West Point and the latter at Louisiana State University, the University of California, and the University of Maryland. The more politically oriented Luis, president of the Congress at the time of his father's death, was constitutionally empowered to fill the presidency in the case of an unexpected vacancy. His more militarily inclined brother, Anastasio, had been head of the National Guard since 1955. When their father was killed, Luis automatically assumed the presidency, while his brother used the National Guard to seize and imprison all civilian politicians who might have taken steps to impede the dynastic succession. In 1957, Luis was formally "elected" to a term that would expire in 1963.

LUIS SOMOZA AND THE PUPPETS: 1957–1967

The decade 1957–1967 bore the mark of Luis Somoza Debayle, a man who seemed to enjoy "democratic" politics and appeared to be committed to the modernization and technical and economic development of his country. The older and wiser of the two Somoza sons, Luis was convinced that in order to preserve the system and protect the family's interests, the Somozas would have to lower their political and economic profile. His ideas and principles fitted neatly with the underlying philosophy and stated objectives of the U.S.-sponsored Alliance for Progress, which was being inaugurated with great fanfare in those years. Many of the programs Luis promoted in Nicaragua—public housing and education, social security, agrarian reform, etc.—coincided with the reform projects of the Alliance.

In politics, Luis attempted to modernize the Liberal party, encouraging dissident Liberals to return to the fold and new civilian leaders to emerge. In 1959 he even had the constitution amended to prevent any member of his family—in particular his intemperate and ambitious younger brother, Anastasio—from running for president in 1963. From the end of his term until his death from a heart attack in 1967, Luis ruled through puppet presidents, René Schick Gutiérrez and Lorenzo Guerrero.

In spite of appearances, however, all was not well during this period. Alliance for Progress developmentalism, while creating jobs for an expanded bureaucracy and providing opportunities for the further enrichment of the privileged, had little positive impact on the lives of the impoverished majority of Nicaraguans, and "democracy" was a facade. Elections were rigged and the National Guard, as always, provided a firm guarantee that there could be no real reform in the political system.

Not surprisingly, therefore, there were a number of attempts to overthrow the system through armed revolt. Some of these attempts were made by younger members of the traditional parties, one was led by a surviving member of Sandino's army, and—from 1961 on—a number of operations were carried out by a new guerrilla organization, the Sandinist Front of National Liberation (FSLN). In response to these "subversive" activities, the dictatorship resorted to the frequent use of the state of siege and Washington helped increase the National Guard's counterinsurgency capabilities.

Though there is no doubt that Luis Somoza disapproved strongly of his younger brother's ambition to run for president in 1967, it is equally clear that there was little he could have done to have blocked it. Anastasio was, after all, the commander of the National Guard. Therefore, in June 1967—after a blatantly rigged election—Anastasio Somoza Debayle became the third member of his family to rule Nicaragua. Luis's death a few months earlier and the bloody suppression of a mass protest rally shortly before the election symbolized the end of an era of cosmetic liberalization and the return to a cruder and harsher style of dictatorship.

ANASTASIO SOMOZA DEBAYLE'S FIRST TERM: 1967–1972

Anastasio differed from his older brother in several important respects. First, whereas Luis had attempted to build up a civilian power base in a rejuvenated Liberal party, Anastasio felt much more comfortable relying simply on military power. As chief of the *Guardia*, he relied on the old tradition of encouraging corruption and protecting officers from prosecution for crimes committed against civilians. In addition, whereas Luis and the puppets had surrounded themselves with a group of highly trained developmentalist technicians (*los minifaldas*, the miniskirts), Anastasio soon began replacing these skilled administrators with essentially unqualified cronies and political allies, many of whom were *Guardia* officers whom Somoza wanted to pay off or co-opt. Finally, whereas Luis had felt that, for the sake of image, the family should consolidate rather than expand its already vast fortune, his younger brother exercised no such restraint in using public office for personal enrichment. The result of all this was that by 1970 Somoza's legitimacy and civilian power base were evaporating rapidly and the government was becoming increasingly corrupt and inefficient.

According to the constitution, Anastasio was to step down from the presidency when his term expired in 1971. The dictator, however, was not bothered by such technicalities. Once in office he quickly amended the constitution to allow himself an additional year in office. Then, in 1971, with the advice and encouragement of U.S. Ambassador Turner Shelton, he arranged a pact with the leader of the Conservative party, Fernando Agüero, whereby he would step down temporarily and hand power over to a triumvirate composed of two Liberals and one Conservative (Agüero, of course) that would rule while a new constitution was written and an election for president was held. The transfer of power, which took place in 1972, was more apparent than real, as Somoza retained control of the guard. The inevitable result was that, in 1974, Somoza was "elected" to another term of office that was formally scheduled to last until 1981.

THE BEGINNING OF THE END: 1972–1977

The half-decade following the naming of the triumvirate in 1972 was a time of mounting troubles for the Somoza regime. Most of the responsibility for the growing systemic crisis lay in the excesses and poor judgment of the dictator himself. Somoza's first major demonstration of intemperance came in the wake of the Christmas earthquake of 1972, which cost the lives of more than ten thousand people and leveled a 600-square-block area in the heart of Managua. Somoza might have chosen to play the role of concerned statesman and patriotic leader by dipping into the family fortune (which, even then, probably exceeded $300 million [U.S.]) in order to help his distressed countrymen. Instead, he chose to turn the national disaster to short-term personal advantage. While allowing the National Guard to plunder and sell international relief materials and to participate in looting the devastated commercial sector, Somoza and his associates used their control of the government to channel international relief funds into their own pockets. Much of what they did was technically legal—the self-awarding of government contracts and the purchasing of land, industries, etc., that they knew would figure lucratively in the reconstruction—but little of it was ethically or morally uplifting.

It was at this point that open expressions of popular discontent with the Somoza regime began to surface. Although the triumvirate was technically in power when the quake struck, Somoza lost no time using the emergency as an excuse to push that body aside and proclaim himself head of the National Emergency Committee. There were many high-sounding statements about the challenge and patriotic task of reconstruction, but it soon became apparent that his corrupt and incompetent government was actually a major obstacle to recovery. The promised reconstruction of the heart of the city never took place. Popular demand for the building of a new marketplace to replace the one that had been destroyed went unheeded. Emergency housing funds channeled to Nicaragua by the U.S. Agency for International Development (AID) went disproportionately into the construction of luxury housing for National Guard officers, while the homeless poor were asked to content themselves with hastily constructed wooden shacks. Reconstruction plans for the city's roads, drainage system, and public transportation were grossly mishandled. As a result, there was a series of strikes and demonstrations as the citizens became increasingly angry and politically mobilized.

It was at this point, too, that Somoza lost much of the support that he had formerly enjoyed from Nicaragua's economic elite. Many independent businessmen resented the way he had muscled his way into the construction and banking sectors. And most were angry at being asked to pay new emergency taxes at a time when Somoza—who normally exempted himself from taxes—was using his position to engorge himself on international relief funds. As a result, from 1973 on, more and more young people with impressive elite backgrounds joined the ranks of the Sandinist Front of National Liberation, and some sectors of the business community began giving the FSLN their financial support.

The second wave of excess followed a spectacularly successful guerrilla operation in December 1974. At that time, a unit of the FSLN held a group of elite Managua partygoers hostage until the government met a series of demands, including the payment of a large ransom, the publication and broadcast over national radio of a lengthy communiqué, and the transportation of fourteen imprisoned FSLN members and themselves to Cuba.[2] Enraged by this affront to his personal dignity, Somoza imposed martial law and sent his National Guard into the countryside to root out the "terrorists." In supposed pursuit of that objective, the guard engaged in extensive pillage, arbitrary imprisonment, torture, rape, and summary execution of hundreds of peasants.

Unfortunately for Somoza, many of the atrocities were committed in areas where Catholic missionaries happened to be stationed. As a result the priests and brothers could—and did—send detailed information about these rights violations to their superiors. The church hierarchy—already displeased with Somoza's decision in the early 1970s to extend his term of office beyond its original legal limit—first demanded an explanation from the dictator and then denounced the guard's rights violations before the world.

Somoza's flagrant disregard for human rights earned him considerable international notoriety. His excesses became the subject of hearings of the U.S. House of Representatives Subcommittee on International Relations[3] and a lengthy Amnesty International investigation.[4] In all, by the middle of the decade, Somoza stood out as one of the worst human rights violators in the western hemisphere.

The year 1977 was a time of mounting crisis for the Somoza regime. That winter, the Episcopal Conference of Nicaragua devoted its New Year's message to a ringing denunciation of the regime's violations of human rights; the U.S.-based International Commission of Jurists expressed concern over the military trial of 111 individuals accused of working with the guerrillas; and Jimmy Carter, who had advocated in his campaign that the United States begin promoting human rights internationally, was inaugurated as president of the United States. Throughout 1977, the Carter administration pressed President Somoza to improve his human rights image. James Theberge, a right-wing, cold war warrior, was replaced as U.S. ambassador to Nicaragua by the more humane and congenial Mauricio Solaún, and military and humanitarian aid was used as a prod in dealing with the client regime. In response to the changing mood in Washington, Somoza, early that year, ordered the National Guard to stop terrorizing the peasantry. In September, he lifted the state of siege and reinstated freedom of the printed press.

Somoza's problems had been compounded in July, when the obese, hard-drinking dictator suffered a near fatal heart attack—his second—and had to be transported to the Miami Heart Institute, where he spent the next one-and-a-half months. This episode stimulated Nicaraguans of all political stripes to consider anew their country's political future. Even Somoza's aides, convinced that he would not return from Miami, began looting the treasury and plotting openly over the succession. As a result, when the dictator did recover, he was faced, upon his return to Nicaragua, with very serious problems within his own political household. Over the next three months he purged many of his former top advisers, including Cornelio Hüeck, president of the National Congress and national secretary of his own Liberal party.

By the last quarter of 1977, the Somoza regime was in deep trouble. Many Nicaraguans were frustrated and disappointed that nature had not been allowed to accomplish a second *ajusticiamiento* the previous summer. With the lifting of the state of siege and the reinstatement of freedom of the press, they could vent their feelings. Newspapers such as Pedro Joaquín Chamorro's *La Prensa* were free to cover opposition activities and discuss in vivid detail the past and present corruption and rights violations of the Somoza regime. In a single week that I spent in Nicaragua early in December, *La Prensa* ran articles on opposition meetings, a successful guerrilla action in the north, the fate of "missing" peasants in guerrilla areas, Somoza's relationship with a blood-plasma exporting firm (Plasmaféresis de Nicaragua), and the apparent embezzlement of AID funds by Nicaraguan Housing Bank officials. As a result, the regime's popular image dropped to an all-time low and Managua was alive with gossip and speculation about the impending fall of the dictator.

This situation undoubtedly emboldened the opposition. In Oc-

tober FSLN guerrillas attacked National Guard outposts in several
cities and towns and a group of prominent citizens—professionals,
businessmen, and clergy who subsequently became known as The
Twelve—denounced the dictatorship and called for a national solution,
which would include FSLN in any post-Somoza government. While
several opposition groups spoke of a dialogue with Somoza, many,
if not most, Nicaraguans felt, as did The Twelve, that

> there can be no dialogue with Somoza . . . because he is the principal
> obstacle to all rational understanding . . . through the long and dark
> history of *Somocismo*, dialogues with the dictatorship have only served
> to strengthen it . . . and in this crucial moment for Nicaragua, in which
> the dictatorship is isolated and weakened, the expediency of dialogue
> is the only political recourse that remains for *Somocismo*.[5]

Even that expediency was to evaporate shortly thereafter in the
reaction to the assassination of Pedro Joaquín Chamorro.

THE WAR OF LIBERATION: 1978–1979

On January 10, 1978, as he was driving to work across the ruins
of old Managua, newspaper editor Pedro Joaquín Chamorro died in
a hail of buckshot fired at close range by a team of professional
assassins. This dramatic assassination was the final catalyst for a war
that culminated in the complete overthrow of the Somoza system
eighteen months later. Though this struggle is often referred to as a
civil war, many Nicaraguans are quick to point out that that term
does not fit because it implies armed conflict between two major
national factions. The Nicaraguan war, they maintain, was actually
a "war of liberation" in which an externally created dictatorial system
supported almost exclusively by a foreign-trained personal army was
overthrown through the concerted effort of virtually all major groups
and classes in the country. Somoza, they say, was simply "the last
marine."

The assassination of Chamorro—a humane and internationally
renowned journalist who, little over three months before, had received
Columbia University's María Moors Cabot Prize for "distinguished
journalistic contributions to the advancement of inter-American understanding"—enraged the Nicaraguan people. Though it is possible
that Somoza may not have been directly responsible for the crime,
few of his countrymen took that possibility seriously. Immediately
after the assassination, angry crowds surged through the streets of
Managua burning Somoza-owned buildings and shouting anti-Somoza

slogans. Later, when it became apparent that the official investigation of the murder was to be a cover-up, the chambers of commerce and industry led the country in an unprecedented general strike that lasted for more than two weeks with 80 to 90 percent effectiveness. Strikes of this sort had almost always proven fatal to Latin American dictatorships; but not so in the case of Anastasio Somoza, for he had the firm support of a thoroughly corrupt military establishment that simply could not afford to risk a change of government. When it became clear that it was hurting the Nicaraguan people more than their well-protected dictator, the strike was called off.

The fact that the strike was over, however, did not mean that Somoza's troubles had ended. To the contrary, Nicaraguans of all classes had experienced the thrill and surge of pride that came with defying the dictator and were, therefore, in no mood to let things slip back to normal. For the next several months, acts against the regime came in various forms. There were daring and quite successful FSLN attacks on National Guard headquarters in several cities, mass demonstrations, labor and student strikes, and—a new factor—civil uprisings in urban areas.

The events of February in Monimbó—an Indian neighborhood in Masaya—were a preview of what was to happen in most Nicaraguan cities that September, when poorly armed civilians rose up against the dictatorship only to be brutally pounded into submission. Fighting in Monimbó broke out between the local inhabitants and the guard on February 10, the one-month anniversary of the Chamorro assassination, and again on February 21, the forty-fourth anniversary of Sandino's assassination. On the second occasion, the inhabitants set up barricades, hoisted banners declaring Monimbó to be a free territory, and held the guard back for almost a week with a pathetic assortment of weapons consisting of homemade bombs, 22-caliber rifles, pistols, machetes, axes, rocks, and clubs. Before it could declare Monimbó "secure" on February 28, the regime had to use a force of 600 heavily armed men backed by two tanks, three armored cars, five 50-caliber machine guns, two helicopter gunships, and two light planes.[6] In the process, the neighborhood was devastated and many dozens, perhaps hundreds, of civilians were either killed outright or arrested and never seen again.

Meanwhile, Somoza was defiantly reiterating his intention to stay in power until the expiration of his term of office in 1981. Swearing that he would never resign before that time, he sputtered angrily at one point that "They will have to kill me first. . . . I shall never quit power like Fulgencio Batista in Cuba or Pérez Jiminéz in Venezuela. I'll leave only like Rafael Leonidas Trujillo of the Dominican

Republic. . . . That is, dead."[7] In a calmer mood on another occasion he commented, "I'm a hard nut. . . . They elected me for a term and they've got to stand me."[8]

The Nicaraguan people, however, were not about to stand Somoza for another two years, much less wait until 1981 to participate in yet another rigged election—the "solution" that the United States, at that time, was promoting. Acts of passive resistance and violent opposition continued. July was a particularly active month. On July 5, The Twelve returned from exile, in defiance of the dictator's wishes, and were greeted as heroes by huge crowds at the airport and throughout the country. On July 19, "over 90% of the businesses in Managua and 70% of those in the country as a whole" answered the Broad Opposition Front's (FAO) call for a one-day, show-of-strength general strike.[9] And, on July 21, Fernando Chamorro, an automobile sales executive, carried out a daring, one-man rocket attack on El Bunker—Somoza's fortified, subterranean office and living quarters—where Somoza was holding a cabinet meeting.

The situation finally came to a head in August. Early that month, the Nicaraguan people heard to their astonishment that Jimmy Carter had sent Somoza a private, but subsequently leaked, letter late in July congratulating him for his promises to improve the human rights situation in Nicaragua. Exasperated by this news and determined to recapture the initiative, the FSLN decided to set in motion plans for its most spectacular guerrilla action to date, the seizure of the National Legislative Palace in the heart of old Managua. According to Eden Pastora, the "Commander Zero" who led the operation, the FSLN had been outraged by Carter's letter. "How could he praise Somoza while our people were being massacred by the dictatorship? It was clear it meant support for Somoza, and we were determined to show Carter that Nicaraguans are ready to fight Somoza, the cancer of our country. We decided, therefore, to launch the people's struggle."[10]

Operation Pigpen, which began on August 22, was as successful as it was daring. Dressed as elite guard of Somoza's son, Anastasio III, twenty-five young FSLN guerrillas, most of whom had never set foot in the National Palace, drove up in front, announced that "the chief" was coming, brushed past regular security personnel, and took command of the whole building in a matter of minutes. Before most of them even realized what was happening, more than fifteen hundred legislators, bureaucrats, and others conducting business in the palace were hostages of the FSLN. It was another humiliating defeat for Somoza. After fewer than forty-eight hours of bargaining the FSLN commandos extracted a stinging list of concessions from the dictator, including $500,000 (U.S.) in ransom, airtime on radio and space in the press for an anti-Somoza communiqué, government capitulation to the demands of striking health workers, and guarantee of safe passage out of the country for fifty-nine political prisoners and the guerrillas. The governments of Panama and Venezuela vied with each other for the honor of providing the FSLN commandos with air transportation and asylum. And thousands of Nicaraguans cheered the new national heroes on the way to the airport as they departed.

The success of the FSLN palace operation triggered massive acts of defiance by Nicaraguan society as a whole. On August 25, the Broad Opposition Front (composed, at that time, of most of Nicaragua's political parties and organizations) demanded Somoza's resignation and declared another nationwide strike, which paralyzed the country for almost a month. Simultaneously, Monimbó-style civil uprisings occurred in cities throughout the country, including Masaya, Matagalpa, Managua, Chinandega, León, Jinotepe, Diriamba, and Estelí. Once again, young people armed only with an assortment of pistols, hunting rifles, shotguns, homemade bombs, and the moral support of their elders erected paving block barricades and battled elite units of Somoza's National Guard. Several towns—including León, the traditional stronghold of Somoza's Liberal party—held out for a week or more against terrible odds.

The outcome, however, was inevitable. Somoza and his hated National Guard knew that they were in a struggle for their very lives. The guard, therefore, fought with unusual ferocity and vengeance, leveling large sections of several cities and taking the lives of between three thousand and five thousand people. The dictator's own son and heir apparent, Harvard-educated Anastasio Somoza Portocarrero, led the ground operations. After first "softening up" insurgent cities and neighborhoods with aerial strafing and bombardment, government troops moved in to "mop up." As most of the active insurgents usually had withdrawn by the time the troops took the cities, the mop-up operations frequently involved the mass summary execution of noncombatants—in particular those males who had the misfortune of being of fighting age.[11]

The events of August and September 1978 caused Nicaraguans on both sides to do some hard thinking. For his part, Somoza apparently began to realize that his dictatorial system might be doomed. In the next ten months, he and his associates worked feverishly to liquidate assets and transfer money abroad. At the same time, however, Somoza displayed an outward determination to hold on and to crush the "Communist . . . jerks." He announced plans to double the size of the guard and bragged openly that, in spite of a U.S. arms freeze, he was having little trouble getting the arms and ammunition he wanted on the open market (mainly from Israel and Argentina).

Somoza was also quite clever in manipulating the United States in his efforts during this period to buy time. The September uprisings had caused the Carter administration, at least temporarily, to feel that Somoza might not be able to survive until 1981. This feeling was accompanied by a growing sense of alarm that Nicaragua might turn into "another Cuba."[12] The dictator played very effectively upon these cold war fears. His lobbyists in Washington argued passionately that Somoza was a loyal ally of the United States, about to be overthrown by Cuban-backed Communists. And from October to January Somoza himself toyed with a U.S.-led mediation team from the Organization of American States (OAS) while it attempted to negotiate a transition agreement between Somoza and the small handful of traditional politicians who were still willing to make deals with the dictator. Dangling the idea of a national plebiscite before the OAS team and his traditional "opponents," Somoza did not kill the mediation process until January 1979, when he apparently was sufficiently confident of his own military strength that he no longer needed such charades.

Ironically, even though the Carter administration reacted with anger to Somoza's treachery by reducing its diplomatic presence in Managua and by finally withdrawing its small team of military attachés, the Americans, too, apparently felt that Somoza had weathered the storm. In May 1979, the administration once again aided the dictator by reversing an earlier position and allowing a $66 million International Monetary Fund (IMF) loan for Nicaragua to be approved without U.S. opposition.

Meanwhile, the Nicaraguan people had also learned some valuable lessons from the events of August and September 1978. It was clear that neither general strikes nor poorly armed mass uprisings would drive Somoza from office. The dictator and his guard had demonstrated their willingness to slaughter and destroy in order to preserve their position. The next uprising, therefore, would have to be led by a larger, well-trained, well-armed guerrilla force. Accordingly, for the next eight months, the Sandinist Front of National Liberation worked to prepare itself for a massive final offensive. The recruitment and training of young men and women—primarily students from urban areas—went on at a frenetic pace as the regular FSLN army expanded from several hundred to several thousand. Members of the opposition—particularly The Twelve—traveled throughout the world explaining the Sandinist cause and soliciting donations. Money received from various governments in Latin America, the Social Democratic parties of Western Europe, and solidarity groups in the United States and elsewhere was used to purchase modern, light, Western-made weapons on the international arms market. In March 1979, the FSLN, which formerly had been divided into three factions, finally coalesced under one nine-man directorate and issued a joint declaration of objectives. The stage was set for the final offensive.

After a false start in Estelí in April, the real final offensive was declared early in June 1979. Paving-block barricades were erected in poor neighborhoods throughout the country and National Guard outposts were overcome one by one as the dictator's control of the country shrank. In mid-June a broad-based government-in-exile was announced by the FSLN. Alarmed by the near certainty of a popular victory, the United States tried various schemes to block such an outcome, including a request to the OAS that a peacekeeping military force be sent to Managua. When this proposal for armed intervention was unanimously rejected, the Carter administration finally began to deal directly with the provisional government. Using various threats and promises, it tried unsuccessfully to force the FSLN to agree to preserve the National Guard—albeit in an altered form—and to include "moderates," such as members of the guard and Somoza's party, in the government. When the FSLN refused, Washington finally

Fighting at the barricades. Ironically, the *adoquín* paving blocks used to construct the barricades had been made in the dictator's own factory. (Photo courtesy of *Barricada*)

accepted the inevitable and arranged for the departure of Somoza to Miami on July 17. A day later, the provisional government took the oath of office in a ceremony held in León and, on July 19, the FSLN entered Managua and accepted the surrender of most of what was left of the National Guard. Ecstatic crowds tore the statues of Anastasio Senior and Luis Somoza from their pedestals and dragged the broken pieces triumphantly through the streets. On July 20, the provisional government entered the capital and appeared in the main plaza to receive the acclaim of a jubilant and grateful people. The Sandinist insurrection had won unconditionally.

THE CONFLUENCE OF GRASSROOTS MOVEMENTS

The overthrow of the Somoza dictatorship had been a product, in large part, of the confluence of two grassroots movements, both having their origins in the 1960s. One of these was Marxist, the other Catholic. The older of the two, the FSLN, was founded in July 1961 by Carlos Fonseca, Silvio Mayorga, and Tomás Borge, former members of the local pro-Soviet Nicaraguan Socialist party (PSN). For these

The Triumph—July 19, 1979.
(Photo courtesy of *Barricada*)

young Nicaraguans, this old Communist party was too Stalinist in organization and too subservient to the Soviet policy of "peaceful coexistence," which in Latin America often meant the docile acceptance of pro-U.S. dictatorships. The founders of the FSLN were determined to create an authentically Nicaraguan revolutionary movement, based on the tactics and sociopolitical objectives of Augusto César Sandino.

For a long time the young rebels were not very successful. At first they attempted to replicate Sandino's tactic of creating a rural guerrilla *foco* (focus) from which to harass the government. In 1967, this tactic led to the disaster of Pancasán in which most of the FSLN's best cadres were surrounded in their *foco* and killed by the National Guard. From then until 1974, the surviving Sandinistas reverted to a strategy of "accumulation of force in silence," temporarily abandoning guerrilla activities and working instead to organize peasants and the urban poor. In 1974, they returned to guerrilla activities, carrying out the successful Managua kidnap-ransom operation mentioned earlier.

The next year, harassed by an enraged Anastasio Somoza, the FSLN split into three "tendencies" in a dispute over tactics. The Prolonged Popular War (GPP) faction was most inclined to follow the Front's original rural *foco* strategy. The Proletarian Tendency (TP) stressed the need to work with and mobilize the urban worker. Neither the GPP nor the TP felt that the time was ripe for an all-out insurrection. In contrast, the Terceristas (Third Force) advocated immediate urban and rural insurrection and a tactical alliance with all anti-Somoza forces, including the bourgeoisie. In the long run, Operation Pigpen and the September 1978 uprisings legitimized the strategy of the Terceristas. By March 1979, the three factions had formally reunited in preparation for the final offensive.

Meanwhile, a very important Catholic effort at mass mobilization was also being waged in the 1970s. Its roots lay in the second Latin American Bishops' Conference held at Medellín, Colombia, in 1968. There the bishops had produced a document condemning the structural inequities of most Latin American social, economic, and political systems and calling for the clergy to make a "preferential option for the poor." Persons of the cloth were urged to organize Christian Base Communities (CEBs), in which Christ's liberating message would be discussed and the poor, who would be told that they, too, were made in the image of God, would be assisted in becoming socially and politically aware and encouraged to demand social justice. To assist the clergy in spreading the "social gospel" and in creating the CEBs, community leaders would be trained as lay Delegates of the Word.

Soon these directives were being implemented throughout Latin

America—even in Nicaragua, where much of the clergy, until the late 1960s, had earned a reputation for being quite conservative. The activities of the lay delegates and the CEBs led to the creation and formation of other grassroots organizations, which mobilized labor, peasants, students, and women. By the mid-1970s, the Somoza regime, which had come to feel threatened by these "subversive" activities, began to strike back, attacking CEBs and, in some cases, murdering lay delegates. This violence radicalized many young Catholics and led some of them to join, or cooperate with, the FSLN.

By 1978, the progressive Catholics and the FSLN were essentially working in tandem in expanding the grassroots organizations and preparing for the final insurrection. The Triumph of July 1979, then, was the product of a joint effort. Accordingly, the revolutionary system that would replace the Somoza dictatorship would be influenced as much by its Catholic humanist roots as by the peculiarly nationalist brand of Marxism of the original founders of the FSLN.

THE NEW REVOLUTIONARY ORDER

The new system was inevitably controversial both at home and abroad. Though ardently nationalist and, in many cases, deeply religious, most Sandinistas were also openly Marxist or Marxist-Leninist in that they found the writings of Marx and Lenin useful in understanding and explaining the history and current condition of Latin America. Consequently, they were automatically viewed with suspicion both by Nicaragua's middle- and upper-class minority— who feared the immediate imposition of a Soviet-style state and economy—and by foreign policy makers in Washington—who were worried about the specter of a "second Cuba." Internally, these fears led to a rapid class polarization, rumor mongering, and a notable lack of cooperation in the reconstruction effort on the part of the private sector. Internationally, especially after the election of Ronald Reagan in the United States, these perceptions produced a multifaceted program to destroy the Sandinista revolution, including a campaign of propaganda and disinformation[13] depicting the government of Nicaragua as a grim, totalitarian Communist regime and an instrument of Soviet expansionism in the Americas. Although most of these allegations were either completely groundless or very nearly so, the U.S. mass media and opposition politicians (perhaps fearing to appear "naive," "liberal," or "biased") rarely challenged the carefully cultivated "conventional wisdom." Reagan's tactics for dealing with the Sandinistas could be criticized but not the administration's picture of the Nicaraguan regime itself.

For U.S. scholars who did research in Nicaragua during this period,[14] the discrepancy between what was heard in the United States and what was seen in Nicaragua proved stark and frustrating. Far from being a coterie of wild-eyed ideologues, the Sandinistas behaved in a pragmatic and, indeed, moderate fashion throughout the first six years. Although they were forced increasingly to rely on the Socialist Bloc for trade and aid, they did not impose a Soviet-style state or a Communist, or even Socialist, economic system. They succeeded in carrying out innovative and highly successful social programs without inordinately straining the national budget. And contrary to the "conventional wisdom," their performance in the area of human rights—though not flawless—would probably rank Nicaragua at least in the top third of Latin American states.[15]

The Sandinistas enjoyed a number of political assets at the time of their victory, but their power was not limitless. Their greatest asset was the fact that their victory had been unconditional. The old National Guard had been defeated and disbanded. The new armed forces were explicitly Sandinist—that is, revolutionary and popularly oriented. What is more, the mass organizations created in the struggle to overthrow the dictator gave the FSLN a grassroots base that dwarfed the organized support of all potential rivals. Finally, the new government enjoyed broad international support. Nevertheless, the country's new leaders were well aware that their revolutionary administration faced certain geopolitical and economic constraints. The Soviet Union had made it clear that it was not willing to underwrite a "second Cuba." Hard currency would not be forthcoming from that source, nor would military support in the event of a U.S. invasion. Furthermore, unlike Cuba, Nicaragua was not an island. Its long borders were highly vulnerable to paramilitary penetration, and any attempt to impose a dogmatic Marxist-Leninist system would certainly have generated a mass exodus of population. Finally, the Catholic Church in Nicaragua was so important and Catholics had played such a crucial role in the War of Liberation that the Sandinistas were neither inclined nor well situated to attack the Catholic traditions of their country. For these reasons it ought not to surprise us that for the next six years the Sandinistas, in fact, attempted to govern in a pragmatic, nonideological fashion.

Sandinista rule was marked by a high degree of consistency and continuity throughout—owing at least in part to the fact that the overall political trajectory of the revolution was set during these years by the same nine-person Sandinista Directorate (DN). Decisions made by DN were based on consensus or near-consensus. Reportedly, important decisions were never made on a 5-to-4 vote. This inherently

conservative style of revolutionary stewardship meant that domestic
and international policy, though adaptive in detail, remained consistent
in overall characteristics and goals. During the entire six years, the
Sandinistas promoted (1) a mixed economy with heavy participation
by the private sector, (2) political pluralism featuring interclass dialogue
and efforts to institutionalize input and feedback from all sectors,
(3) ambitious social programs, based in large part on grassroots
voluntarism, and (4) the maintenance of diplomatic and economic
relations with as many nations as possible regardless of ideology.

However, in spite of such overarching continuity, it is possible
to divide this period into three subperiods that were clearly conditioned
by the country's international environment. The first, which lasted
until the election of Ronald Reagan in November 1980, was a time
of euphoria and optimism. The second, spanning the nearly two years
from that election to the spring of 1982, was a period of growing
awareness of, and concern with, the hostile intentions of the new
administration in Washington. In the third, during the little over three
years that had elapsed from the spring of 1982 through the summer
of 1985, Nicaragua would meet the full brunt of an unprecedentedly
massive surrogate invasion, direct CIA sabotage, and economic strangulation.

The first year was the quiet before the storm. Jimmy Carter was
still president of the United States. Though not pleased with the
Sandinista victory, his administration had decided to make the best
of it, offering economic aid with strings attached in the hopes of
manipulating the Sandinistas in a direction acceptable to conservative
Washington. During this period, the FSLN consolidated the revolution
politically, by promoting the growth of grassroots organizations,
reorganizing the Sandinista armed forces, and reequipping them with
standardized military matériel. Much of the latter was obtained from
the Socialist Bloc: The United States had earlier refused an arms
purchase request by the Sandinistas. Nevertheless, the Sandinista
Army was quite small (15,000–18,000 soldiers) and the civilian militia—little more than an association of patriotic marching units—
barely constituted even a credible addition to the country's defensive
force.

In economic affairs, the Sandinistas decided to honor Somoza's
foreign debt in order to maintain Nicaraguan creditworthiness in
Western financial circles. Lengthy negotiations with the international
banking community led to concessionary terms for repayment. Public
loans and aid poured in from a wide variety of countries. And,
although the government immediately confiscated properties owned

by the Somozas and their accomplices, it respected the rest of the private sector and even offered it substantial financial assistance.

In line with the decision to preserve a large private sector, the revolutionaries also created an interim government in which all groups and classes in society, including the privileged minority, could have a voice. The plural executive (Junta of National Reconstruction), created shortly before the victory, included wealthy conservatives as well as Sandinistas. The interim legislative body (Council of State) gave corporative representation to most parties and organizations of significance in Nicaraguan society. This was also a time of ambitious social programs—most notably the 1980 Literacy Crusade, which was carried out at relatively low cost to the government owing to its ability to mobilize massive voluntary participation.

The period was not without tension, however. Class polarization had set in almost immediately. Many in the minority privileged classes were certain that totalitarian communism was just around the corner. Accordingly, some fled immediately to Miami while others first illegally decapitalized their industries, transferred money abroad, and then fled. Moreover, a crisis of sorts occurred early in 1980, when conservatives on the Junta resigned in a pique over the fact that the organizations representing their class had been given representation on the new Council of State which was only slightly more than equivalent to the minority percentage that they represented in the population as a whole. At the same time, the independent daily, *La Prensa*, was taken over by a conservative wing of the Chamorro family, and from then on it was to take a highly critical position, playing to the fears of the privileged classes.

On balance, however, these were not bad times. Other conservatives were found to replace those who had resigned from the Junta. Human rights in general were respected. And *La Prensa* was allowed to make scurrilous and frequently false attacks on the system with virtual impunity. Former Somoza military personnel and accomplices were subjected to legal investigation and trial rather than execution. Indeed, the death penalty itself was immediately abolished.

The second period, one of growing concern and apprehension, began in the fall of 1980 with the election of Ronald Reagan. That summer the Republican party platform had "deplor[ed] the Marxist-Sandinista takeover of Nicaragua" and had promised to end all aid to that country. Campaign aides to Reagan had advised using on Nicaragua the full gamut of techniques (e.g., economic destabilization, surrogate invasion) employed by the United States in the past to destroy Latin American regimes of which Washington did not approve. In fact, the new administration wasted little time in implementing

these suggestions. Early in 1981, U.S. economic assistance to Nicaragua
was terminated and the administration began to allow anti-Sandinista
paramilitary training camps to operate openly in Florida, California,
and the Southwest.[16] That December, President Reagan signed a
directive authorizing the CIA to spend $19.8 million to create an exile
paramilitary force in Honduras to harass Nicaragua.[17] Although some
counterrevolutionary (*contra*) attacks occurred as early as 1981, such
activity increased markedly in 1982, as bridges, oil-refining facilities,
and other crucial infrastructure, in addition to civilian and military
personnel, were targeted. That same year, too, the United States used
its central position in the World Bank and the Inter-American Development Bank (IDB) to cut off the flow of badly needed multilateral
loans to Nicaragua.

This growing external threat was clearly reflected in Nicaragua
in increased class polarization, greater emphasis on austerity and
defense, and some—albeit still relatively mild—government infringements on human rights. The acceleration of class polarization began
almost immediately after the Reagan victory. Now, many in the
privileged classes apparently saw even less need than before to
accommodate themselves to the new revolutionary system. Within
days of Reagan's victory, representatives of the Superior Council of
Private Enterprise (COSEP) walked out of the Council of State. On
November 17, Jorge Salazar, vice-president of COSEP and head of
the Union of Nicaraguan Farmers (UPANIC), was killed in a shoot-
out with state security forces while allegedly meeting with gun
runners in preparation for armed counterrevolutionary activities. Even
though the government televised highly damaging evidence against
him, Salazar immediately became a martyr for the privileged classes.

From then on, tension mounted steadily as the conservative
church hierarchy, the opposition microparties, COSEP, and *La Prensa*—
all working in obvious coordination with the U.S. Embassy—showed
less and less inclination to engage in constructive dialogue and an
ever greater tendency to obstruct and confront. This behavior, in turn,
generated resentment by the masses. In March 1981, for instance,
Sandinista Defense Committees (CDSs) "in effect challenged the
authority of the Ministry of the Interior by [staging demonstrations]
blocking plans by the opposition MDN [Nicaraguan Democratic Move-
ment] to hold a political rally [at Nandaime] that had been presented
by the government as proof that pluralism was still viable in Nicaragua."[18]

In addition, an increased emphasis was placed on military
preparedness. The Sandinista Army was almost immediately expanded
to around 24,000 persons, the level at which it would stay until 1983.

Recruitment and training for members of the militia was stepped up markedly and obsolete Czech BZ-52 ten-shot rifles were imported to arm them. Socialist Bloc tanks, anti-aircraft equipment, helicopters, and troop transport vehicles were also imported. Moreover, there was talk of obtaining Soviet MiG fighter jets. This buildup, however, was clearly defensive, as noted in a staff report of the House Committee on Intelligence, when, in September of 1982, it chastized the U.S. intelligence community for making dramatic public statements about Nicaragua's offensive intentions and capabilities while, at the same time, secretly briefing high-level administration officials to the contrary.[19] Meanwhile, there was a general belt-tightening as the importation of non-essential goods was restricted and salaries were held down.

All of the government social programs were continued. Indeed, in 1981, over 70,000 young people participated in a voluntary primary health crusade. But, overall, the people of Nicaragua were beginning to feel the negative effects of the Reagan assault on their country.

Finally, as is true in all states in time of war or threat of war, certain human rights were gradually infringed upon in the name of national security. Late in 1981, in response to *contra* activity in the region, the government ordered the involuntary evacuation of some 8,500 to 10,000 Miskito Indians from isolated communities along the Río Coco. Although careful investigations into this matter indicate that the evacuation itself was carried out in a humane fashion, some isolated incidents occurred during subsequent security activities on the Miskito Coast in which individual commanders or soldiers disobeyed orders to respect the lives of prisoners and were apparently responsible for the execution or permanent "disappearance" of up to 150 individuals.[20] Also apparent was a deterioration in the right to due process for political prisoners in general, and on the Miskito Coast in particular. Finally, on a half-dozen occasions, *La Prensa* was closed for two-day periods. This action was taken under the terms of a press law decreed by the original Junta (of which, ironically, *La Prensa* owner Violeta Chamorro had been part)—a law calling for such action in the event that an organ of the media was found to have disseminated material that was not only false *but also* destabilizing. However, even with these shutdowns, *La Prensa* continued to operate freely and in bitter opposition to the government more than 95 percent of the time. Moreover, at no point during this period did human rights infringements in Nicaragua even remotely approach the wholesale abuses prevalent in a number of other Latin American countries. In fact, late in 1982, the U.S. ambassador to Nicaragua, Anthony Quainton (a Reagan appointee), admitted candidly to a group of which I was a part that the human rights situation there was better than in El Salvador or Guatemala—ironically two countries that Washington was then trying to portray as having made great strides in this respect.

The third period, from early 1982 through mid-1985, might aptly be labeled "weathering the storm." The "storm," in this case, was the Reagan administration's massive and multifaceted campaign to destabilize and overthrow the Sandinista government, which, by the onset of this period, was "covert" in name only. The CIA-coordinated recruitment, training, arming, and disgorging of *contras* into Nicaragua had escalated rapidly from the force of 500 originally envisioned in the CIA finding of late 1981 to over 15,000 by 1984 (a proportionately equivalent invasion of the United States would number over 1,280,000). Direct involvement by CIA personnel was also evident in the destruction of Nicaraguan oil-storage facilities late in 1983 and the mining of Nicaraguan harbors early in 1984. Furthermore, ever-larger numbers of U.S. military personnel participated in nearly continuous, highly menacing joint military maneuvers in Honduras and in naval "exercises" off both Nicaraguan coasts.

Accompanying these military and paramilitary efforts was an escalating program of economic strangulation. Washington continued to block approval of Nicaraguan loan requests before the World Bank and the IDB. U.S. trade was at first drastically curtailed (the Nicaraguan quota for exporting sugar to the United States was cut by 90 percent in May 1983) and then, in May 1985, embargoed completely. Washington also made an effort, albeit an only partially successful one, to pressure its allies to follow suit.

These activities had a clear impact on Nicaragua, though not always one that U.S. policy makers would have desired. In economic matters the country was hurt, but by no means brought to its knees. Although the economy grew steadily under Sandinista rule (except in 1982, when a severe flood occurred, followed by drought), problems inherited from Somoza, combined with a sharp decline in the world prices of Nicaragua's export commodities and the enormous direct and indirect cost of the *contra* war, meant that by this third period Nicaragua was having increasing problems in servicing its debt. Accordingly, Venezuela ceased (1983) and Mexico drastically curtailed (1984) supplies of oil to the country. As a result, by 1984 and 1985 the Sandinistas were forced to turn to the USSR for most of their petroleum needs. The scarcity of foreign exchange also meant severe shortages of imported goods, or of products manufactured in Nicaragua from imported materials or with imported machinery. Of course, such shortages also triggered rampant inflation and spiraling wage demands, which could not be satisfied given the tremendous diversion of government revenues into defense.

Social services were also negatively affected. As increased emphasis was placed on defense, government spending on health, education, housing, food subsidies, and so on, had to be cut back. Further, it is clear that the *contras* were deliberately targeting the social service infrastructure. Many government employees in health, education, and cooperatives were kidnapped, tortured, and killed; schools, clinics, day-care centers, and grain-storage facilities were destroyed. However, if all of this activity was designed to so damage the living standards of most Nicaraguans that they would become angry with their government and ultimately overturn it, someone had badly miscalculated. Although the human condition did decline during this latter period, support for the government actually appears to have grown—as measured by levels of membership in pro-Sandinista grassroots organizations.[21] In the aftermath of the Triumph (1979-1980), membership reached a peak of about 250,000–300,000 persons. Thereafter, it declined for a couple of years—as a result, perhaps, of apathy or a sense of lack of fulfillment of unrealistically high expectations for the revolution. However, by late 1982, grassroots membership had begun to climb again and, by 1984, it had doubled or tripled over the previous highwater mark. By then, around half of all Nicaraguans aged 16 or older were in such voluntary support organizations.[22] Clearly the intervening variable was the *contra* war, the effects of which really began to hit home late in 1982. Simply put, Nicaraguan's had come together to support their government in this time of national emergency and foreign threat.

The same period also witnessed a significant buildup in the military. Nicaragua stepped up its purchase of military hardware such as helicopters, propeller-driven aircraft, artillery, anti-aircraft equipment, troop transports, and light weaponry—mainly from the Socialist Bloc (the United States had applied pressure to dissuade other potential suppliers such as France). By 1983 or 1984, the Sandinista Army, which had held constant at around 24,000 strong since 1981, increased to over 40,000; in addition, a military draft was instituted. At the same time, the Sandinista Militia—a lightly trained body of over 60,000 civilian volunteers who had previously been armed with liberated Somoza-era weaponry and obsolete Czech BZ-52 rifles— was largely reequipped with Socialist Bloc AK-47 automatic rifles. This increased preparedness (in combination with the fact that, in Nicaragua itself, the *contras* had little political support) paid off. The *contras* proved incapable of achieving even their most minimal objective

A Sandinista militiawoman and friends, La Trinidad, December 1983. In mid-1985 a large force of contras took and temporarily held La Trinidad, killing several dozen townfolk. (Photo by the author)

of seizing and holding a Nicaraguan population center that could be declared the seat of a new government.

At first, the political response of the Sandinistas to the external threat was predictably defensive. In the spring of 1982, following *contra* attacks on important Nicaraguan infrastructure and the disclosure in the U.S. media of President Reagan's earlier authorization of funding for CIA-sponsored paramilitary operations against their country, the government declared a state of prewar emergency under which certain civil and political rights were temporarily suspended. Some measures (such as the short-term preventive detention of suspected "subversives") had actually begun during the previous period; others (such as precensorship of the printed media) were new. The implementation of these measures was relatively mild. The short-term preventive detention measure affected only a few hundred persons at any one time. And *La Prensa*, though now heavily censored, at least continued to function. (In El Salvador the only real opposition papers had long since been driven completely out of business through the murder or exile of their owners.)

Another new political measure, decreed in July 1982, was the massive decentralization of government. Under it, the country was divided into six "Regions" and three "Special Zones" for all governmental functions. The main purpose of this reform was to avoid the stifling effects of centralized bureaucratic control by creating institutions for local decision making and public policy implementation; another important objective was to institute a system of government that could continue functioning even if communications were badly disrupted or if Managua were occupied by enemy troops.

Eventually, however, as more and more Nicaraguans rallied around their government, the Sandinistas came to show renewed confidence in the people and to take a more relaxed approach to domestic politics. Late in 1983, the government actually passed out many tens of thousands of automatic weapons to civilians so that they could help defend their families, farms, villages, and neighborhoods. Meanwhile, the government, in consultation with all political parties and groups that chose to enter into dialogue, had been working to create a mechanism to implement the Sandinistas' oft-repeated promise to hold general elections. Eventually, in September 1983, and with considerable opposition input, a political parties law was hammered out and enacted. Three months later the government announced that the elections would be held in 1984. Early in 1984, November 4 was set as the exact date and, in March, an electoral law modeled after "key components of the French, Italian, Austrian, and Swedish electoral systems,"[23] was enacted. The Reagan administration denounced the Nicaraguan election in advance as a "Soviet-style farce," hyped businessman Arturo Cruz (whom they apparently knew had no intention of running) as the only viable opposition candidate, and reportedly pressured certain other candidates to withdraw from the contest at the last moment. Nevertheless, the election did take place as scheduled, and, though either ignored or panned by the U.S. media, it was certified as being a meaningful, clean, and relatively competitive election (given the difficult circumstances under which it was held) by a number of observer delegations representing Western European parliaments and governments, the U.S.-based Latin American Studies Association, and so on.[24] Although voting was not obligatory, 75 percent of those registered (93.7 percent of the voting-age population had registered) cast ballots. Although three parties each to the right and the left of the FSLN appeared on the ballot, the Sandinistas captured 63 percent of the vote. That gave the presidency and vice-presidency to Daniel Ortega and Sergio Ramírez, and 61 of the 96 seats in the new (constituent) National Assembly to the FSLN.

The elected government was formally inaugurated in January 1985. But there was little time or cause for celebration. In the United States during most of November, news of the Nicaraguan election had been effectively drowned in intensive media coverage of several skillfully timed Reagan administration "leaks" to the effect that Soviet-built MiG jets might be en route by ship to Nicaragua. Although these allegations proved utterly groundless, they effectively raised to a feverish pitch the paranoia of the American public over the "Nicaraguan menace." Subsequently, Washington unilaterally broke off the bilateral talks being conducted with Nicaraguan diplomats. Then, in February 1985, Reagan admitted that it was the objective of his administration to dismantle the Sandinista power structure unless the Sandinistas decided to cry "uncle."[25] In sum, as of mid-1985, there were no signs that an end to the suffering of the Nicaraguan people was anywhere in sight.

NOTES

1. Rigoberto López Pérez as quoted in Mayo Antonio Sánchez, *Nicaragua Año Cero* (Mexico: Editorial Diana, 1979), p. 96.

2. For an FSLN account of this action and a transcript of the communiqué, see Comando Juan José Quezada, *Frente Sandinista: Diciembre Victorioso* (Mexico: Editorial Diogenes, S.A., 1976).

3. U.S., Congress, House Committee on International Relations, Subcommittee on International Organizations, *Human Rights in Nicaragua, Gua-*

temala and El Salvador: Implications for U.S. Policy, hearings, June 8, 9, 1976 (Washington, D.C.: U.S. Government Printing Office, 1976).

4. Findings summarized in *Amnesty International Report, 1977* (London: Amnesty International Publications, 1977), pp. 150–153.

5. *Apuntes para el Estudio de la Realidad National*, no. 1 (Junio 1978), p. 9.

6. Ibid., p. 22.

7. "Somoza Rules out Early Departure," *Central America Report*, vol. 5, no. 12 (March 20, 1978), p. 95.

8. "The Twelve: Nicaragua's Unlikely Band of Somoza Foes," *Washington Post*, July 23, 1978.

9. "Nicaragua Strike," *Central America Report*, vol. 5, no. 29 (July 24, 1978), p. 231.

10. "Rocking Nicaragua: The Rebels' Own Story," *Washington Post*, September 3, 1978, p. C-1.

11. Organization of American States, Inter-American Commission on Human Rights, *Report on the Situation of Human Rights in Nicaragua* (Washington, D.C.: General Secretariat of the OAS, 1978).

12. For more detailed analysis of U.S. policymaking in this period, see William LeoGrande, "The Revolution in Nicaragua: Another Cuba?" *Foreign Affairs*, vol. 58, no. 1 (Fall 1979), pp. 28–50; and Richard R. Fagen, "Dateline Nicaragua: The End of an Affair," *Foreign Policy*, no. 36 (Fall 1979), pp. 178–191.

13. For some specific examples of the use of disinformation against Nicaragua see Thomas W. Walker, "The Nicaraguan-U.S. Friction: The First Four Years, 1979–1983," in Kenneth M. Coleman and George C. Herring, eds., *The Central American Crisis* (Wilmington, Del.: Scholarly Resources Inc., 1985), pp. 181–186.

14. The present author had the privilege of working with several dozen such scholars while editing *Nicaragua in Revolution* (New York: Praeger Publishers, 1982) and *Nicaragua: The First Five Years* (New York: Praeger Publishers, 1985).

15. Throughout the first six years, the Nicaraguan government invited various human rights monitoring organizations to conduct investigations in Nicaragua. Consequently, there are a number of extensive reports on human rights under the Sandinistas. Most are critical of certain violations, but the abuses they identify are relatively mild compared to those of many other Latin American states. See Amnesty International, "Nicaragua Background Briefing: Persistence of Public Order Law Detentions and Trials" (London: AI, 1982); Amnesty International, "Prepared Statement of Amnesty International USA on the Human Rights Situation in Nicaragua Before the Subcommittee on Human Rights and International Organizations," U.S. House of Representatives, September 15, 1983 (mimeograph); Inter-American Commission on Human Rights, Organization of American States, *Report on the Situation of Human Rights of a Segment of the Nicaraguan Population of Miskito Origin* (Washington, D.C.: OAS, 1984); and America's Watch, *Human Rights*

in Nicaragua (New York: America's Watch, 1984). America's Watch eventually confronted the stark discrepancy between what the Reagan administration was charging and what these reports state, in America's Watch, *Nicaragua: Reagan, Rhetoric and Reality* (New York: America's Watch, 1985).

16. The story of the *contra* training camps first became public via Eddie Adams, "Exiles Rehearse for the Day They Hope Will Come," *Parade Magazine* (March 15, 1981), pp. 4–6.

17. "U.S. Plans Covert Operations to Disrupt Nicaraguan Economy," *Washington Post*, March 10, 1982, and "U.S. Said to Plan 2 C.I.A. Actions in Latin Region," *New York Times*, March 14, 1982.

18. Jack Child, "National Security," in James D. Rudolph, ed., *Nicaragua: A Country Study* (Washington, D.C.: U.S. Government Printing Office, 1982), p. 202.

19. See page 142 (note 18) in Chapter 7.

20. Inter-American Commission on Human Rights, *Report on the Situation of Human Rights*.

21. My estimates of grassroots organization memberships are rough. They are based on conversations held during ten visits to Nicaragua with individuals working in mass mobilization, and on Luis H. Serra, "The Sandinista Mass Organizations," in Walker, ed., *Nicaragua in Revolution*, pp. 95–114, and Luis H. Serra, "The Grass-Roots Organizations," in Walker, ed., *Nicaragua: The First Five Years*, pp. 65–89.

22. Interestingly, this estimate is essentially corroborated by an in-house U.S. Embassy estimate for late 1984, which places grassroots membership at 7–8,000,000. This information was revealed by an official in the U.S. Embassy to a group of which I was a part on June 25, 1985.

23. Latin American Studies Association (LASA), *The Electoral Process in Nicaragua: Domestic and International Influences* (Report of the Latin American Studies Association Delegation to Observe the Nicaraguan General Election of November 4, 1984), Austin, Tex.: LASA, 1984, p. 29.

24. LASA, *The Electoral Process*; Thom Kerstiens and Piet Nelissen (official Dutch Government Observers), "Report on the Elections in Nicaragua, 4 November, 1984" (photocopy); Irish Inter-Party Parliamentary Delegation, *The Elections in Nicaragua, November, 1984* (Dublin: Irish Parliament, 1984); Parliamentary Human Rights Group, "Report of a British Parliamentary Delegation to Nicaragua to Observe the Presidential and National Assembly Elections, 4 November, 1984" (photocopy); and Willy Brandt and Thorvald Stoltenberg, "Statement [on the Nicaraguan elections in behalf of the Socialist International]," Bonn, November 7, 1984.

25. "After Reagan's 'Uncle' Policy, Managua Announces 'Flexibility,'" *Latin American Weekly Report* (March 1, 1985), p. 1.

4

The Economic Dimension

When the revolutionary government that replaced the Somoza regime in 1979 drew up its first comprehensive economic plan—*The 1980 Program for Economic Reactivation in Benefit of the People*—it was well aware that it faced a stark reality. "We are confronting," the government observed, "the effects of a hundred years of dependent capitalism which expresses itself in the appropriation of the national wealth by an extremely small group, leaving the vast majority of the population in misery and ignorance."[1] The term *dependent capitalism* as used in this statement is not a rhetorical or demogogic expression. It refers to an objective reality—a socioeconomic pattern predominant throughout Latin America that seems to persist whether the political form of the moment be liberal "democracy" (for example, Colombia from the late 1950s on), one-man dictatorship (the Dominican Republic under Rafael Trujillo or Venezuela under Marcos Pérez Jiménez), progressive military rule (Peru, 1968–1975), or rightist military dictatorship (Brazil 1964–1985, or Chile after 1973).

There is a profound difference between what is loosely called free enterprise or capitalism in the United States and its counterpart in Latin America. Capitalism in the United States coexists with relatively high levels of social justice precisely because it is dependent on the bulk of the American people as consumers. Most of what U.S. industry produces is consumed in the United States. The economic system, therefore, would collapse if the majority of citizens were exploited to the extent that they could no longer consume at relatively high levels. Quite the opposite is true in Latin America, where the so-called "capitalist" economies are overwhelmingly externally oriented, placing great emphasis on the production of products for export. Under these dependent capitalist systems the common citizen is important as a cheap and easily exploitable source of labor rather than as a consumer. Therefore, there is little or no economic incentive for the privileged classes that dominate most Latin American governments to make the sacrifices necessary to improve the conditions of the majority of the people.

While prerevolutionary Nicaragua was not at all unusual as an example of a society distorted by dependent capitalism, it was nevertheless an exceptionally and strikingly tragic case. Unlike certain other countries—such as Bolivia, where natural resources are in relatively short supply—Nicaragua is, and always has been, a land of impressive economic potential. The population/land ratio is very favorable. Not only is Nicaragua the largest of the Central American countries, it is the least densely populated, with just over 20 persons per square kilometer as opposed to 45 for the region as a whole and approximately 210 for El Salvador. The land itself is rich and varied, with different soil, climatological, and altitude characteristics suitable for the production of a wide variety of crops and livestock. The country's many rivers and volcanos offer easily exploitable sources of both hydroelectric and geothermal energy, and internal waterways facilitate inexpensive domestic transportation and present the possibility of exploitation as part of some future transoceanic waterway. Nicaragua has both Caribbean and Pacific coastlines, providing direct access not only to the food and mineral resources of the seas but also to the major markets of the world. The country has significant timber resources—from pine forests in the highlands to hardwood stands in the lowland tropics. Among the known mineral assets are silver and, particularly, gold. Finally, the Nicaraguan people, with their relatively homogeneous culture and language and their indomitable spirit and *joie de vivre*, are themselves a very important national asset.

The tragedy—indeed the gross injustice—of prerevolutionary Nicaragua was that in spite of all this potential and some apparent signs of "development," such as frequent spurts in gross national product (GNP), the vast majority of the Nicaraguan people, even in the late 1970s, led a stark existence while a small, privileged minority monopolized and misused the national resources to their own nearly exclusive benefit. This fact is illustrated by income distribution figures for the late 1970s that show that 20 percent of the population (i.e., the upper and middle class) received 60 percent of the national income while 80 percent (the lower classes) were expected to make do with the other 40 percent. The poorest 50 percent had access to only 15 percent of the national income, for an average of a little more than a couple of hundred dollars per person per year.[2]

EVOLUTION OF THE ECONOMIC SYSTEM

The best way to understand the inequities of the Nicaraguan economic system is to examine its historical roots. Nicaraguan economic history prior to the Sandinist Revolution is divisible into four distinct time spans: (1) the colonial period, from the 1520s to the 1820s; (2) the first half century of independence, from the 1820s through the 1870s; (3) the period of primitive dependent capitalism, from the late 1870s through the 1940s; and (4) the rise of modern dependent capitalism, from the 1950s through the 1970s.

The Colonial Economy

When the Spaniards arrived in western Nicaragua in the early sixteenth century they found a relatively advanced agrarian society. The approximately one million native inhabitants of the region—descendants of colonizers and refugees from the Mayan and Aztec civilizations to the north—lived in villages and cities ranging in population from a few hundred to tens of thousands. This was a feudal society, with chiefs, subchiefs, and commoners, in which tribute flowed from the lowly to the lofty. However, land was held collectively and each inhabitant of the villages and cities had access to a designated plot nearby. The rich soils of the region yielded agricultural products in abundance ranging from corn, cassava, and chili to beans, tobacco, and a variety of vegetables. Each population center had one or more local markets at which agricultural products were sold. Though periodic crop failure and intertribal warfare undoubtedly inflicted occasional acute hardship, the economy in general was relatively self-sufficient and self-contained. The market system, intraregional trade, and general access to rich agricultural lands provided the material wherewithall for the satisfaction of basic human needs.

The Spanish conquest, as I noted earlier, had an immediate and devastating impact on this economic system. Superimposing themselves on the existing feudal structure, the *conquistadores* demanded tribute in gold and, when that was depleted, Indian slaves. Within a few decades the near total destruction of the native population through death by contact with European diseases and the export of slaves created a severe manpower shortage that all but destroyed the labor-intensive agricultural base of the region's economy. To be sure, some lands remained under intensive cultivation throughout the colonial period, providing some export products such as corn and cacao and food to meet the region's much reduced internal demand. But, for the most part, the rich lands of Nicaragua reverted to jungle or were exploited for the raising of cattle to produce hides, tallow, and salted meat for sale to other colonies.

In a few decades, therefore, the economy had become essentially externally oriented. In addition to the sale of corn, cacao, and cattle products, the tiny Spanish elite accrued wealth through the exploitation of forest products, shipbuilding, and intermittent gold mining—all to

meet external rather than internal demands. The underpopulation of
the colony and the concentration of wealth in the hands of the
privileged classes of León and Granada made Nicaragua a prime
target for attacks by pirates from England and elsewhere in Europe,
further contributing to the region's status as a colonial backwater.
The process of underdevelopment had begun.

The First Half Century of Independence

The partial interruption of foreign dominance resulting from
the disintegration and eventual collapse of Spanish colonial rule in
the early nineteenth century was reflected in important changes in
the Nicaraguan economic system. It is true that British traders were
quick to provide the landed elite with an outlet for their traditional
export products, but the relative political anarchy and international
isolation of the first half century of independence also encouraged
the growth of a number of other types of economic activity. There
was a rapid growth in the number of self-sufficient peasant farms or
huertas. A fragile, indigenous marketing system was reestablished.
And, in the villages and cities, various types of cottage industry
began to develop.

For most of the Nicaraguan people this economic system, though
certainly not highly developed, was fairly benign. Although he may
have been exaggerating slightly, one observer writing in the early
1870s noted that "peonage such as is seen in Mexico and various
parts of Spanish America does not exist in Nicaragua. . . . Any citizen
whatever can set himself up on a piece of open land . . . to cultivate
plantain and corn."[3]

Primitive Dependent Capitalism

The relative isolation of Nicaragua and the gradual development
of an internally oriented economy were abruptly interrupted by the
coffee boom that hit Central America in the late 1800s. Coffee was
probably introduced into the country as an exotic curiosity in the
first quarter of the nineteenth century. By 1848 it was being produced
commercially on a small scale. In the early 1850s it was a favorite
beverage of the twenty thousand or so foreign passengers each month
who utilized Cornelius Vanderbilt's Accessory Transit Company route
across Nicaragua on their way to California.[4] But it was not until
the 1870s that coffee really came into its own. By then the international
demand was so strong that the country's ruling elite was motivated
to monopolize and redirect much of Nicaragua's productive capacity
toward the cultivation of that one export product.

Two factors of crucial importance to the production of coffee are fertile land in the right climatological setting and a large, essentially unskilled work force that can be called upon to offer its services for a few months during the harvest season. In Nicaragua in the early 1870s both were in short supply. The coffee culture had already moved into most of the exploitable lands around Managua, and other promising lands in the northern highlands were occupied by independent peasants and members of Indian communes engaged in traditional subsistence farming. And as the rural masses had access to their own land, there was no pool of vulnerable and easily exploitable peons.

The traditional elite solved both of these problems with ingenuity and speed. In the late 1870s and 1880s they took the land they coveted and created the work force they needed through a combination of chicanery, violence, and self-serving legislation. Individual squatter farmers and Indians working the land through communal arrangements were extremely vulnerable to legal manipulation because, in most cases, these people held rights to the land by tradition rather than by legal title. For several decades the agrarian elite had attempted, through legislation, to abolish communal and squatter landholdings. In 1877, under the presidency of Conservative Pedro Joaquín Chamorro, an agrarian law was passed that outlawed communal holdings and gave individuals the right to buy "unoccupied" national lands. The resulting massive dislocation of Indian communal farmers and individual peasants led inevitably to the War of the Comuneros of 1881 in the Pacific and north-central regions of Nicaragua. After a series of cruel battles in which as many as five thousand Indians may have been killed,[5] the new order was imposed on the region. Coffee was free to expand into new land.

The laws that forced the small farmer off the land also helped create a vulnerable rural proletariat. To reinforce this phenomenon the elite-controlled governments also passed laws against "vagrancy" and the cultivation of plantain—the banana-like staple food of the peasants.[6] Obliged to buy staples at high prices in the plantation commissaries, many coffee workers were forced to rely on credit from these company stores. Before long they were trapped into a very effective system of debt peonage. In less than a decade, the self-sufficient peasantry of a large section of the country had been converted into a dependent and oppressed rural proletariat. Most rural Nicaraguans began to lead a life of insecurity, fluctuating between the good times of the coffee harvest, from November through February, and the hardship and unemployment of the *tiempo muerto* (dead period) between harvests.

The growth of the coffee culture also marked the birth of

dependent capitalism in Nicaragua. Before this period the economy was based on traditional cattle ranching and subsistence peasant and communal farming. Neither involved a significant use of capital. Coffee, however, was different. First, years before the first harvest, the planter had to make a significant investment in preparing the land and planting and nurturing the seedlings. When the trees began to bear fruit, it was necessary to spend considerable sums of money on manpower and machinery. A large work force was needed for the handpicking of the coffee berries, and more people and machinery were employed in weighing, pulping, drying, sorting, sacking, and transporting the product.

It is not surprising, then, that although some small farmers converted to coffee bean production, most of those who went into this new enterprise were large landholders, prosperous commercial speculators, and, in some cases, foreigners. The Conservative oligarchy used its control of the legislative process to pass the Subsidy Laws of 1879 and 1889, which gave planters of all nationalities cultivating more than five thousand trees a subsidy of five cents per tree.[7] Among other things, these laws encouraged foreign colonists to seek their fortunes on the fertile slopes of the central highlands. With them came an infusion of new capital.

Once established as the cornerstone of the Nicaraguan economy, coffee held that position until the 1950s. This is not to say that other forms of agriculture were completely wiped out. Some farsighted peasants chose to flee the new coffee zones entirely, moving on to subsistence farming on land in other regions that were not yet coveted by the landed elite. In addition, the traditional precapitalist cattle *hacienda* (ranch) of the lowlands, though now less important, was by no means completely eclipsed. But overall, coffee was clearly the mainstay of the country's economy.

With the growth of the coffee industry, Nicaragua developed what is often loosely referred to as a "banana republic" economy— one based heavily on a single primary export product. Typically, the benefits of the system flowed heavily to a small domestic elite and its foreign trading partners. Taxes on coffee profits, which might have helped redistribute income to the impoverished majority, were virtually nonexistent. The common citizen was an abused instrument of production rather than a beneficiary of the system. The Nicaraguan economy also became subject to periodic "booms" and "busts" produced by the fluctuation of the world price of its single product. In good times the economy grew and coffee planters imported luxury goods and machinery, invested money abroad, and educated their children in the United States and Europe. The first of the Somoza dictators received his U.S. education as a result of such a boom. In bad times, such as those following the onset of the 1929 Depression, coffee prices plummeted and the economy stagnated. Planters hunkered down, lived off savings and investments, and imported fewer luxury items and less machinery.

Typical also of the banana republic syndrome was the fact that throughout most of the period little effort was made by the governments of Nicaragua to see that the economy served the purpose of genuine national development. The notable exception to this rule was the regime of Liberal strongman José Santos Zelaya from 1893 to 1909. Zelaya had no real quarrel with laissez faire economics or with coffee. Indeed, he helped the coffee industry by opening up "new" lands and improving Nicaragua's transportation network. Nevertheless, he also emphasized education, brought fiscal responsibility to the government, created the rudiments of a modern administrative structure, and insisted on national economic self-determination. His refusal to concede to the United States canal rights that would have diminished the economic and political sovereignty of his country and his subsequent negotiation with other powers for a more equitable canal treaty contributed to the U.S. decision to encourage, and then reinforce militarily, the Conservative rebellion of 1909. After Zelaya, the Conservatives, and later the much-chastened Liberals, provided governments whose economic policies fit the banana republic model closely. Within a few years of their ascent to power, the Conservatives gave their U.S. protectors essentially the same canal treaty Zelaya had rejected. The United States had no intention of building a Nicaraguan canal. It simply wanted to buy up the rights in order to preclude the possibility that any other country would do so. From then until the 1950s virtually no effort was made to alter Nicaragua's established role as a provider of a single primary product.

Modern Dependent Capitalism

The quarter century preceding the War of Liberation was a time of economic modernization and dependent "development." New products were added to Nicaragua's portfolio of exports, technology and technocrats became faddish, the government bureaucracy grew rapidly, expanding—at least on paper—into various social service areas, and the gross national product grew in respectable spurts. But the benefits of this change and growth did not "trickle down" to most Nicaraguans. Their perilous standard of living remained essentially constant as the gap between them and the tiny middle and upper classes widened relentlessly.

One of the most obvious changes to occur during this period

was the diversification of Nicaragua's exports. In addition to coffee and beef products, Nicaragua now exported significant quantities of cotton, sugar, bananas, wood, and seafood. The most important new product was cotton. The sharp increase in the world price of this raw material in the early 1950s, flowing out of heightened demand during the Korean War, motivated Nicaraguan planters and speculators to invest in cotton production in the Pacific lowlands. Nicaragua, which had exported only 379 metric tons of cotton in 1949, increased that figure to 43,971 metric tons in 1955. Eventually as much as 80 percent of the cultivated land on the Pacific coast was converted to cotton.[8] Some cattle ranches became cotton plantations, but, as in the case of the coffee boom seven decades earlier, much of the land that went into the production of this new export product was appropriated in one way or another from peasant producers of grains and domestic staples. Once again independent farmers were transformed into a rootless rural proletariat in the name of "progress" and "development" for the privileged few.

Cotton, like coffee, was subject to cycles of boom and bust. The first period of bust began in 1956, three years after the end of the Korean War. Compared with coffee, cotton was a very capital-intensive activity. It required great investments in machinery, fertilizer, insecticides, and labor. In Nicaragua's case, cotton came to account for almost all of the tractors and harvesters, most of the irrigation systems, and more than three-fourths of the commercial fertilizer used in the country.[9] Small-scale production of cotton was simply out of the question.

Another factor that affected the Nicaraguan economy in this period was the birth of the Alliance for Progress in the early 1960s. A U.S.-sponsored response to the revolutionary success of Fidel Castro in Cuba, the alliance was designed to bring about social and economic development in Latin America through politically moderate means. Enlightened reform from above would, it was hoped, defuse the "threat" of popular revolution from below. The Somozas and the traditional elite of Nicaragua found the idea of the alliance very appealing. Not that they were particularly concerned with its lofty objectives of social and economic justice. Rather, they saw it in more practical terms as a legitimizing device and a source of a variety of economic opportunities. In return for rather painless paper reforms and the creation of a modern social-service bureaucracy, they would receive increased foreign aid and technological assistance and have access to numerous new business opportunities.

Nicaragua in the 1960s was typified by a peculiar type of neopositivism reminiscent of Mexico in the days of Porfirio Díaz.

Technology, foreign investment, and "development"—as defined in terms of growth in gross national product—were the new articles of faith. A group of highly trained developmentalists known as the technocrats or, less respectfully, the "miniskirts," were elevated to positions of great responsibility. The heart of their operations was the Banco Central in downtown Managua. There the dictator-president, the head of the "miniskirts" (Francisco "Ché" Láinez, the bank's director), and the cream of Nicaragua's technocratic community met late into the night planning the country's economy as if they were the board of directors of a large corporation. Feasibility studies were ordered, foreign investment was wooed, and joint ventures were embarked upon. Once a year the Banco Central issued an annual report brimming with tables and analyses concerning the national economy. To help train even more business technocrats, Harvard University's School of Business Administration cooperated in the creation of the Central American Institute of Business Administration (INCAE), located in the outskirts of Managua.

A parallel stimulus for capitalist development in Nicaragua, which coincided with the Alliance for Progress, was the birth of the Central American Common Market in 1960. This attempt at regional economic integration provided increased incentive for both incipient industrialization and the diversification of export products. As such it was, for a while, an additional boon to the privileged domestic and international groups who controlled these activities. However, the Soccer War of 1969, between El Salvador and Honduras, brought about the demise of this integrative effort.

The developmentalist optimism of the 1960s proved to be a hollow illusion. Compared with the rest of Latin America, Nicaragua received relatively little foreign investment—perhaps because doing business in that country normally entailed paying off the Somozas in one way or another. Though economic growth did take place, its benefits were concentrated in relatively few hands. The Somozas and their allies simply used their control of the expanded governmental apparatus and the country's new technocratic expertise to increase their own fortunes. Eventually, in the late 1960s and early 1970s, the technocrats themselves were pushed aside as the corrupt and intemperate Anastasio Somoza Debayle replaced skilled administrative personnel with National Guard officers and other cronies to whom he owed rewards for personal loyalty.

The problem of corruption had existed throughout the Somoza period. Anastasio Somoza García had encouraged corruption in his subordinates as a way of isolating them psychologically from the people and thus making them dependent on him. Although the corporate image of the Somoza system improved during the developmentalist years of Luis and the puppets, official corruption continued unabated. In a conversation in 1977, Luis Somoza's close adviser and confidant, Francisco Láinez, the chief of the "miniskirts" during that earlier period, told me an interesting story. One day Luis Somoza, in a pensive mood, asked Láinez to tell him in all frankness what one thing he, Láinez, would do, if he were in Luis's shoes, to bring development to Nicaragua. Láinez thought for a moment and then responded that he would take each of the major categories in the national budget—health, education, etc.—and see to it that *at least half* of that money actually went for the purposes for which it was ostensibly destined. According to Láinez, Luis simply smiled sadly and responded, "You're being unrealistic."[10] This is not to say that, at the highest levels, money was being stolen openly. That would not have been acceptable to Washington—which was footing much of the bill—nor was it necessary, since the Somozas' absolute control of the government gave them the ability to apply a legalistic patina to the flow of public funds. Even after the patent and massive misuse of international relief funds following the 1972 earthquake, the U.S. government, intent on not embarrassing a good ally, was able for several years to produce audits that appeared to refute claims that these funds had been misappropriated.

A final important economic phenomenon of this last prerevolutionary period was the emergence of three preponderantly powerful economic groups each composed of an assortment of influential firms, individuals, and families with financial operations rooted in distinct major banking systems. The function of these groups seems to have been to pool influence, expertise, and financial power in such a way as to give group members an economic advantage over nonmembers. The negative impact on society was that, by reducing competition, they tended to contribute to "a greater inequality of both power and wealth."[11]

The oldest of the groups had its roots in the first half of the twentieth century. Clustered around the Banco de América, this so-called Banamérica Group was originally probably an economic response by Conservative Granada-based families and firms to the vagaries of doing business in a country dominated by a dictator from the other party. Whatever its early roots, the Banamérica Group burgeoned into a powerful association of interests and firms including sugar, rum, cattle, coffee, export-import businesses, department stores, and supermarkets. Banamérica's international banking ties were with the Wells Fargo Bank and the First National Bank of Boston.

A second group, clustered around the Banco Nicaragüense,

emerged in the 1950s and 1960s as an apparent response to the Banamérica Group. With a clearer identification with León and the Liberal tradition, the BANIC Group included coffee and cotton interests, a major beer industry, merchants and commercial enterprises, land development and construction, and lumber, fish, and vegetable oil processing. BANIC's major banking ties were with the Chase Manhattan Bank.

The third important group was that of the Somozas. It consisted of the family's wide holdings in practically every segment of the economy. For several decades its banking needs had been covered by the national banks—first the Banco Nacional and then the Banco Central. These banks frequently extended loans to the Somozas that would not have been available to private citizens and that often were never repaid. Though it probably was not necessary, the Somoza group eventually set up its own bank, the Banco Centroamericano.

Interestingly, the Somoza financial empire in prerevolutionary Nicaragua—though vast and impressive—was less clearly recognized as a "group" than were the BANIC and Banamérica networks.[12] This was probably due to the fact that Somoza interests defended themselves not through their group association per se, but rather through the family's direct control of the government and all of its institutions. The founder of the dynasty, Anastasio Somoza García, acquired many of his agrarian properties at the outset of the Second World War by simply taking over the numerous coffee plantations and cattle ranches that the government confiscated from German landholders. In addition he used his unchallengeable coercive power to acquire other prime properties by simply making Mafia-style "offers that couldn't be refused" to the hapless owners. He and his sons also used their control of the government to pass legislation favorable to their agrarian and business interests, to avoid taxes, to award themselves lucrative contracts, and to create obstacles for economic competitors and political adversaries.

Though the Somoza financial empire had the reputation of being poorly and inefficiently run, this was more than compensated for by the tremendous advantage it enjoyed through direct control of government. By the time the dynasty was overthrown the family had accrued a portfolio worth well in excess of $500 million (U.S.)—perhaps as much as one or one-and-a-half billion dollars. The Somozas owned about one-fifth of the nation's arable land and produced export products such as cotton, sugar, coffee, cattle, and bananas. They were involved in the processing of agricultural products. They held vital export-import franchises and had extensive investments in urban real estate. They owned or had controlling interests in two seaports, a maritime line, the national airline, the concrete industry, a paving-block company, construction firms, a metal extruding plant, and various other businesses including Plasmaféresis de Nicaragua, which exported plasma extracted from whole blood purchased from impoverished Nicaraguans. Finally, the Somozas had huge investments outside Nicaragua ranging from real estate and other interests in the United States to agricultural enterprises throughout Central America to textiles in Colombia. Shortly before their overthrow, they even bought controlling interests in *Visión*, the Latin American equivalent of *Newsweek* or *Time* magazines.

The events of the 1970s accentuated the abuses and defects of the Nicaraguan economic system. In the last years of the Somoza dynasty, it had reached a state that, from the point of view of most citizens, was intolerable. For over a century, the country's rich natural resources had been plundered, appropriated, and abused for the benefit of a tiny minority. Millions of Nicaraguans had become economic instruments rather than fulfilled and participating human beings. Public revenues and foreign aid officially destined "to meet basic human needs"[13] had been routinely laundered to end up in the pockets of the ruling family and its allies. The nation's public and private banks had been used first as instruments for the concentration of wealth and finally as conduits for the export of capital as the erstwhile ruling class began to flee into exile. The War of Liberation of 1978–1979 was as much a product of systemic socioeconomic factors as it was an expression of intense political opposition to a particularly venal dictator.

SANDINIST ECONOMIC POLICY

The economic policy and programs of the revolutionary government that took power in July 1979 constituted a radical departure from those of previous regimes. Nicaragua's new political leaders, though varied in their ideological and social backgrounds, were remarkably united in their sense of historic responsibility and their determination to carry out a social revolution rooted in a New Sandinist Economy that, they said, would "make possible *a just, free, and fraternal human life in our fatherland.*"[14] Intensely aware of the tremendous human costs of the old patterns of dependent capitalism, they were determined to fashion an economic system that would not only eradicate past abuses but also transfer the "center of attention" from the privileged minority to the exploited "masses." Significantly, however, the economic tactics they adopted during the first six years were pragmatic and in no way rigidly tied to any preconceived ideology. The Sandinistas made no attempt to impose a socialist economic system, much less a Communist one.

One of the first signs of the pragmatic, nonorthodox nature of Sandinista economic policy was the decision, taken by the Sandinistas at the time of the Triumph, to honor Somoza's onerous $1.6 billion foreign debt. Although they had absolutely no moral obligation to pay for the dictator's scandalous misuse of international funding, the new government realized that servicing "Nicaragua's" financial obligations was necessary if the country were to remain creditworthy in international financial circles. Therefore, unable to pay according to the schedule worked out with Somoza, they immediately entered into a long process of negotiation with a group of private banks to which Somoza owed $580 million and ultimately won a more realistic repayment plan. Then, "between 1980 and 1982, Nicaragua made every interest payment . . . , a record almost unparalleled anywhere in Latin America in those crisis-ridden years."[15] Only in 1983, when it simply became impossible to continue all payments as scheduled, did Nicaragua begin to prioritize the servicing of some debts while renegotiating others.

A further indication of pragmatism in international economic policy was the Sandinistas' decision to adopt a policy of "walking on four legs" in the development of aid and trade relations with the rest of the world. The objective was to actively pursue economic relations with four groups of countries: the Socialist Bloc, the United States, other developed countries, and the Third World. Accordingly, we find that from 1978 to 1982, Nicaraguan exports to and imports from the Socialist Bloc rose from 0 and 1 percent, respectively, to 7 and 11 percent of the Nicaraguan relationship with the world. By mid-1985, the overall value of trade with the Socialist Bloc stood at 20 percent. For the United States, equivalent figures were 23 and 31 percent (1978), 24 and 19 percent (1982), and an overall 17.5 percent just before the 1985 trade embargo. For the rest of the developed world the tally was 38 and 25 percent (1978), 43 and 22 percent (1982), and an overall 36 percent in mid-1985. Finally, for the Third World, equivalent statistics were 39 and 43 percent (1978), 26 and 47 percent (1982), and an overall 26.5 percent in mid-1985.[16] In other words, throughout the first six years, Nicaragua maintained a diversified trade policy. Even at the end of this period, only about one-fifth of its world trade was with the Socialist Bloc.

Diversity was also the rule in the areas of aid and credit. Throughout its first six years, the new government sought and received assistance from a wide variety of countries. The major disappointment, of course, was the United States, which, immediately after Ronald

Reagan's inauguration in 1981, cut off all economic assistance to Managua. However, very few other countries followed the U.S. lead. Throughout the ensuing years, Nicaragua received assistance from such politically disparate states as Argentina, Austria, Brazil, Canada, Denmark, Libya, Mexico, Peru, Sweden, and various countries in the Socialist Bloc (to name just a few). Indeed, when the Reagan administration declared its full trade embargo in 1985, a variety of countries immediately expressed their disapproval by offering additional assistance or credit. Significantly, such assistance was about evenly balanced between the Socialist Bloc and Yugoslavia ($202 million) and Western Europe ($198 million).

The Sandinistas also demonstrated pragmatism in the domestic sphere with their decision not to socialize the Nicaraguan economy completely. Such a move would have been counterproductive, as the public sector already faced a severe shortage of trained manpower due to the inevitable flight into exile of many members of the middle class and the already greatly expanded role of the state. Furthermore, the Cuban experience of oversocialization served as a useful negative example. It is true that all of the properties of the Somozas and their accomplices were immediately confiscated, making the people the collective owner of 20 percent of the arable land, numerous industrial and commercial enterprises, and thousands of private homes and mansions. In addition, the government nationalized the banking and insurance systems—the latter because it was unable to cope with the needs of a war-ravished country, and the former so as to block the continued flight of capital abroad and to direct loans to those segments of the economy in which they could have the greatest impact. Moreover, in the ensuing years some other properties were nationalized for reasons of overriding national interest or because the owners underutilized, decapitalized, or otherwise abused their rights. However, during each of the six years of Sandinista rule, the private sector accounted for between 50 and 60 percent of the gross domestic product (GDP).

The government demonstrated its determination to preserve the private sector by taking several important measures. Especially in the first few years, it made considerable sums of money available in the form of loans to capitalists willing to reactivate their enterprises. It also provided key private producers access to foreign currency at low rates of exchange. It quickly established the *ley de Amparo* (Law of Protection), which provided Nicaraguan citizens the right to seek redress for and question the legality of the everyday activities of the government (including the confiscation of property). And, beginning in 1983, it issued "guarantees of inexpropriability" for rural properties being efficiently utilized.

It is true that figures showing production by the private sector of a relatively constant 50–60 percent of GDP mask certain important changes that were taking place *within* that sector. A few urban enterprises—such as the luxurious Club Terraza in Managua, which the government confiscated and put under worker ownership and management, and certain large private rural properties that were seized and subsequently turned into peasant cooperatives or parceled out to individual small farmers—were still part of the private sector, even though the nature of ownership had changed significantly. Yet, overall, traditional private property was normally respected as long as the owner obeyed the law and remained productive.

Behind such flexibility and pragmatism, however, was the Sandinistas' determination to control Nicaragua's mixed economy in such a way as to serve the interests of all Nicaraguans. Pursuing what they described as "the logic of the majority," the Sandinistas immediately set up a state monopoly over the sale of export products in order to channel a substantial part of the earnings from exports into badly needed social and economic infrastructure. They also tightly controlled imports in order to conserve scarce foreign exchange for high-priority social and economic inputs. In addition, they issued and enforced laws for the protection of urban and rural workers and peasants renting parcels from large landholders. Finally, they used the influence and financial leverage of the state to promote the production of greater quantities of basic food products.

The economic problems facing the new government during these years were awesome. The Somozas and their accomplices had left Nicaragua with a $1.6 billion foreign debt (in per capita terms, the highest in Latin America) and another $0.5 billion in war damages. Adding insult to injury, they had also pilfered the banking system of all but about $3 million. The world market value of almost all of Nicaragua's export products declined sharply from 1980 onward. In 1982, the country suffered the most costly natural disaster in its recorded history—extensive flooding followed by drought. And finally, starting in the early days of the Reagan administration, the new government faced an elaborate U.S.-orchestrated program of economic destabilization, which featured the severance of economic aid; the curtailment and, in 1985, the complete embargo of all U.S.-Nicaraguan trade; attempts to create an international economic boycott; the blocking of loans from international lending organizations such as the World Bank and the Inter-American Development Bank; the use of *contras* to inflict infrastructural and crop damage and to necessitate the

The 1981 cotton harvest. The chronic labor shortage at harvest time, aggravated in 1981 by a bumper cotton crop and greater economic security for the agrarian lower classes, necessitated the mobilization of volunteer labor from among a variety of groups, including urban blue- and white-collar workers (*top*) and the Sandinist Popular Army (*bottom*). (Photos by the author)

Ruined grain storage facility. Built by the new government as part of its effort to insure more universal access to food, this depository in Ocotal—destroyed in June 1984—was but a fraction of the hundreds of millions of dollars worth of social and economic infrastructure destroyed by the contras as of mid-1985. (Photo by the author)

divergence of scarce funds into defense; and the direct use of the CIA to destroy oil-storage facilities at Corinto (1983) and to mine Nicaragua's harbors (early 1984).[17]

It should not be surprising, therefore, that the Nicaraguan economy was in markedly worse shape in the mid-1980s than it had been at its prerevolutionary highwater mark in 1977. But when the Kissinger Commission argued in January of 1984 (1) that Sandinista economic performance had been "poor" and (2) that this alleged bad performance had been due in part to "mismanagement invariably associated with regimes espousing Marxist-Leninist ideology,"[18] it was engaging in clever sophistry. The Sandinistas had clearly not used Marxist-Leninist ideology in their economic planning. What is more, Kissinger's use of 1977 as a base year was deliberately deceptive. Although Nicaragua's per capita GDP *had* declined around 38 percent from 1977 through 1983, it had actually *risen* by 7 percent overall in the years 1980, 1981, 1982, and 1983. Kissinger had been able to show a decline *only* by including two years of economically devastating civil conflict during which the Sandinistas were not even in power! Furthermore, even though a 7 percent per capita GDP growth over a period of four years would not ordinarily be impressive, it was not bad when compared with the negative 14.7 percent registered for Central America as a whole during the same years.[19] Indeed, Nicaragua had not merely the best growth rate in Central America but one of the best in all of Latin America—and this in spite of the very formidable array of economic problems mentioned earlier.

This relatively strong economic performance appears to have been the product of various factors. In the first place, with its low population density, rich lands, and industrious people, Nicaragua had always been a country of considerable economic potential. Previously bottled up by the corrupt, inefficient, and elitist Somoza system, this potential could now be more fully realized. It is not surprising that total production of most agricultural products—both domestic and export—rose to or exceeded prewar levels within a few years after the ouster of the dictator. The new government was even successful in stimulating the production of nontraditional export products such as castorseed, garlic, ginger, onions, mangoes, melons, peanuts, and sesame seed, which by 1983 accounted for 10 percent of the total value of exports.[20]

The second possible reason for such growth may be the practical, nonideological behavior of the Sandinistas themselves. Instead of engaging in "guerrilla economics," they had preserved a mixed economy and had carefully weighed alternatives in making economic decisions. These measures not only bore fruit in the domestic economy but also gave the Sandinistas a moderate image abroad, thus enabling them to build trade and aid relationships with a wide variety of countries. In short, although the Sandinistas made their share of mistakes and failed to convince the country's bourgeoisie to cooperate as fully as would have been desirable, under the circumstances they did pretty well.

By 1985, Nicaragua's economic future was unclear. In the previous year, the GDP had actually begun to decline. By 1985, the foreign debt had risen to over $4 billion (U.S.). Both the war and the U.S. policy of economic destabilization were taking their toll. Farming in the war zones had been disrupted; over 180,000 displaced persons were in need of government care; hundreds of millions of dollars of economic infrastructure had been destroyed; U.S. manufactured machinery in gold mines, on farms, or in urban factories and offices lay idle for lack of spare parts; and over 40 percent of the national budget was being diverted to the war effort. Obviously, no economy on earth could withstand this type of pressure forever. But Nicaraguans in general—long accustomed to suffering—were facing their problems with dogged determination.

NOTES

1. Ministerio de Planificación, *Programa de Reactivación Económica en Beneficio del Pueblo* (Managua: Secretaría Nacional de Propaganda y Educación Política del FSLN, 1980), p. 98.

2. Ibid., p. 99.

3. Paul Levy as quoted in Jaime Wheelock Román, *Imperialismo y Dictadura: Crísis de una Formación Social* (México: Siglo Veintiuno Editores, 1975), p. 29.

4. David Richard Radell, *An Historical Geography of Western Nicaragua: The Spheres of Influence of León, Granada, and Managua, 1519–1965* (Ph.D. dissertation, University of California, Berkeley, 1969), p. 188.

5. Wheelock Román, *Imperialismo y Dictadura*, p. 77.

6. Ibid., p. 71.

7. Radell, *An Historical Geography*, p. 202.

8. Wheelock Román, *Imperialismo y Dictadura*, pp. 125, 126.

9. Ibid.

10. From a lengthy conversation with Francisco Láinez in his home in Managua during the second week of December 1977.

11. Harry Wallace Strachan, *The Role of the Business Groups in Economic Development: The Case of Nicaragua* (D.B.A. dissertation, Harvard University, 1972), p. 7.

12. Ibid., pp. 16, 17.

13. A favorite expression of U.S. officials during the Carter administration.

14. Ministerio de Planificación, *Programa de Reactivación Económica*, p. 11. The emphasis is in the original.

15. Sylvia Maxfield and Richard Stahler-Sholk, "External Constraints," in Thomas W. Walker, ed., *Nicaragua: The First Five Years* (New York: Praeger Publishers, 1985), p. 258.

16. The 1978 and 1982 statistics are from "Lunes Socio-Económico," *Barricada*, May 23, 1983; those for 1985 are from "Reagan Wields a Double-Edged Trade Sword," *Central America Report*, vol. 12, no. 17 (May 10, 1985), p. 129.

17. For more details about the U.S. destabilization effort see Maxfield and Stahler-Sholk, "External Constraints," and Thomas W. Walker, "Nicaraguan-U.S. Friction: The First Four Years, 1979–1983," in Kenneth M. Coleman and George C. Herring, eds., *The Central American Crisis: Sources of Conflict and the Failure of U.S. Policy* (Wilmington, Del.: Scholarly Resources, 1985), pp. 157–189.

18. Kissinger Commission, *Report of the National Bipartisan Commission on Central America* (Washington, D.C.: U.S. Government Printing Office, 1984), p. 30.

19. For the sources behind these statistics as well as an excellent discussion of the economic model followed by the Sandinistas and the overall results, see Michael E. Conroy, "Economic Legacy and Policies: Performance and Critique," in Walker, ed., *Nicaragua: The First Five Years*, pp. 219–244.

20. Maxfield and Stahler-Sholk, "External Constraints," p. 252.

5

Culture and Society

When the outsider travels for the first time in Central America he or she may expect—as I did on my first trip in 1967—to find relatively similar little countries. After all, could a handful of contiguous ministates with little geographic extension, tiny populations of a few million each, and a long history of colonial and early postcolonial union be much different from one another? But they could be, and they are. Undoubtedly, the unique character of original native populations, varying climatological influences, and dissimilar patterns of colonization and economic exploitation all had something to do with Central America's variety. Whatever the causes, the individuality of each country is striking indeed. Nicaragua, for instance, is practically as different from the neighbors with which it shares borders (Costa Rica and Honduras) as it is from those with which it does not (Guatemala and El Salvador). The uniqueness lies more in the areas of cultural traits and national character than in social patterns and structures.

CULTURE

Nicaraguan culture is rich and fascinating. In an obvious sense it is part of the wider Hispanic American culture. Like other Latin Americans, most Nicaraguans speak Spanish, are at least nominally Roman Catholic, and place great importance on the family and the defense of personal *dignidad* (dignity). Yet, embedded in this matrix of Hispanic universality are various traits that Nicaragua shares with only a few other countries or exhibits in complete isolation.

Language is an area in which Nicaraguans have their own special qualities. Unlike most other Latin Americans, they rarely, if ever, use the standard *tú* form of informal address. Instead, like the Argentines, a few Colombians, and some peoples on their borders, they address each other with the archaic, nonstandard, informal pronoun *vos* and modify the person of their verbs to fit. Soon after the Sandinist victory, customs officials were busily stamping each incoming passport with an exuberant colloqial greeting that translates: "Nicaragua awaits thee (*vos*) with the smile of lakes and volcanos and the brilliant and dignifying sun of liberty."

Nicaraguan language is also spicy. One regional song that is practically the functional equivalent of a national anthem ends with the phrase, "Long live León, *jodido!*" *Jodido* and forms drawn from the same root (to screw), unacceptable for use in mixed company elsewhere in Latin America, are an almost essential condiment in Nicaraguan speech. People of all classes and both sexes revel in the appropriate use of pungent vocabulary, double entendre, and off-color jokes. Little is off limits to the irreverent tongue of the fun-loving Nicaraguan. In the old days, the Somozas themselves were the brunt of hundreds of jokes. Priests and Americans have always been favorite targets. And since the Sandinist victory, Nicaragua's new leaders have been mercilessly roasted.

Nicaraguan vocabulary also includes a number of words of non-Spanish origin. Place names and forms used for common rustic items such as green peppers, corn, and turkey reflect the lingering influence of Nicaragua's ancient Indian heritage. On the other hand, the many years of U.S. occupation have left their linguistic impression in the form of numerous adopted English words. To use just one example, when I hitchhiked from the Honduran border to Managua in July 1979, I was, as the Nicaraguans put it, going by "ride."

On a more serious plane of verbal expression, Nicaragua has evolved a rich literary tradition. At the turn of the century, a young native poet, Rubén Darío, won international acclaim as the founder of Latin America's first clearly original literary movement, "modernism." To this day, his birthplace is preserved as a national shrine, and poets and writers in Nicaragua are held in particularly high esteem. Darío was followed in the first half of the twentieth century by a number of writers: Santiago Argüello (prose, poetry, and drama); Gustavo Alemán-Bolaños (novels, poetry, and political tracts); and Salomón de la Selva (poetry). More recently, the poet Pablo Antonio Cuadra, who examines the essence of things *nica* in his famous book *El Nicaragüense* (*The Nicaraguan*), distinguished himself as a contributor to the columns of *La Prensa* and as the editor of the prestigious literary journal *El Pez Y La Serpiente* (*The Fish and the Snake*). Pedro Joaquín Chamorro, the martyred editor of *La Prensa*, also turned his talents to creative literature. Shortly before his assassination in 1978, Chamorro produced a volume of short stories and two novels, *Richter*

7 (which depicts the decadence of the Somoza system and the tragic erosion of Nicaraguan culture in the period of "reconstruction" following the earthquake of 1972) and *Jesús Marchena* (dealing with, and written in the colloquial language of, the dispossessed rural poor).[1] Another contemporary writer-philosopher, José Coronel Urtecho, emerged from a conservative background to become a highly respected intellectual catalyst for the War of Liberation and an important revolutionary poet thereafter. Also on the left was the famous priest, Ernesto Cardenal, who won international acclaim as a revolutionary poet before joining the FSLN forces as a pastor in the field and subsequently serving as minister of culture in the revolutionary government. Numerous other leaders of the revolutionary government—among them Interior Minister Tomás Borge and Vice President Sergio Ramírez—also turned their hand to prose or poetry.

Similarly, Nicaraguans have made notable contributions in the fields of art and music. There is a rich indigenous artistic heritage dating back to precolonial times that currently manifests itself in the pottery, leatherwork, woodcarving, embroidered clothing, and other handicrafts available in local public markets. On a more sophisticated plane, the National School of Fine Arts, founded in Managua in the early 1940s, produced a number of well-known figures including the abstract painter Armando Morales. In the area of music, Nicaragua also has its formal and folk components. The outpouring of popular revolutionary music generated by the War of Liberation was particularly interesting. Pressured by the Carter administration to improve his human rights image by allowing limited freedom of expression, Somoza relaxed his censorship of radio broadcasts slightly in the year before his fall. As a result, some radio stations devoted considerable air time to thinly veiled or openly revolutionary music. In a very real sense, the haunting and inspiring tunes and lyrics of such revolutionary singers and composers as Carlos Mejía Godoy became the background accompaniment of the young people who fought at the barricades.

Nicaraguans also exhibit their cultural uniqueness in their religious ceremonies. Like Catholics throughout Latin America, the inhabitants of each Nicaraguan city and village hold annual festivities honoring patron saints. But unlike the people of any other Latin American country, Nicaraguans have a week-long celebration for the Immaculate Conception of Mary. The festivities of *La Purísima*, which culminate on December 8, far outshadow other holidays, including Christmas. During *La Purísima*, altars to the Virgin are erected or decorated in homes or workplaces throughout the country and the people of each neighborhood or village, especially the children, go from altar to altar singing songs and reciting prayers. For their piety, they are rewarded with small gifts—usually edible—that normally include a piece of sugar cane. Even in the wake of the War of Liberation—a time of great economic hardship—Nicaraguans of all classes and political persuasions celebrated *La Purísima* with tremendous enthusiasm. Indeed, one of the most moving sights I saw in that period was that of two teenaged war heroes, dressed in FSLN battle fatigues, standing enraptured in front of a tiny home altar— their Belgian automatic rifles temporarily abandoned on the floor like children's playthings.

Another delightful aspect of Nicaraguan culture is the cuisine. Again, there are elements of both the universal and the particular. Like Mexicans and other Central Americans, Nicaraguans eat corn in the form of *tortillas*. *Tortillas* vary in size, color, and thickness from country to country. In Nicaragua they are large, thin, and made of finely milled white corn. They are often used as an edible utensil in which to wrap barbecued meat, beans, or whatever one happens to be eating. Another absolutely essential item in Nicaraguan cookery is beans. As elsewhere in Latin America—since most people cannot afford the regular consumption of animal protein—beans serve as the main source of protein. The small red bean to which Nicaraguans are particularly addicted is refried with rice to produce a delicious dish called *gallo pinto* (spotted rooster)—a favorite breakfast food of people of all classes. Like many other Latin Americans, *nicas* also enjoy *tamales*. Their *nacatamal*, however, has its own particular character. Wrapped in a pungent leaf from a banana-like plant rather than a corn husk, it consists of corn *masa* (dough), rice, tomatoes, potatoes, chili, cassava root, and often a small piece of meat. Another very typical Nicaraguan dish is *vaho*, which is prepared by slowly steaming salted meat and various vegetables in layers over the same banana-like leaves in a large covered container. In general, Nicaraguan cuisine is well worth trying. Though usually tastefully seasoned, it is seldom hot. For lovers of "hot stuff," however, a bottle or bowl of fine, lip-mummifying *salsa de chile* (chili sauce) is seldom very far away.

No discussion of food would be complete without some mention of drink. The favorite nonalcoholic beverage in Nicaragua is coffee— the best (very good, indeed) coming from the high country around Matagalpa. Like other Latin Americans, Nicaraguans who can afford it drink their coffee 50-50, with hot milk, at breakfast and black with sugar during the rest of the day. Other typical sweet drinks are made from toasted cacao and green or toasted corn. In the field of alcoholic beverages Nicaragua excels. The typical lightly alcoholic drinks are beer and the more traditional and indigenous *chicha*, made from fermented corn mash. The favorite hard liquor is rum, of which Nicaragua has one of Latin America's very best, *Flor de Caña* (Flower of the Cane).

In all, Nicaraguan culture is rich, varied, and unique. Ironically, however, one of the many sins of the Somozas and their accomplices was to ape and promote foreign culture—especially North American— at the expense of that which was authentically *nica*. Not surprisingly, the preservation and strengthening of Nicaraguan culture was a high priority of the FSLN when it seized power. Their determination in this respect was signaled immediately by the creation of the Ministry of Culture, housed, ironically, in one of the deposed dictator's former residences, El Retiro. Before long, there was also a Sandinista Association of Cultural Workers (ASTC) which, in addition to advancing the interests of people in the plastic and performing arts, also worked in promoting Nicaraguan culture. The Ministry, the ASTC, and other groups and individuals did much in the next six years to stimulate a burgeoning of cultural expression. Small museums were created, performing groups (such as the national circus) were encouraged, an award-winning movie industry came into being, mural art flourished, a huge annual exhibition and sale of hand-crafted children's toys, *la Piñata*, became a Managua Christmas tradition, and new cultural journals (such as *Nicaráuac*, published by the Ministry of Culture) were printed. Even on Sandinista television, inexpensive foreign programming was gradually giving way to relatively expensive but more appropriate locally produced material. Under Somoza, 95 percent of the programming had been foreign—mainly of U.S. origin. However, in 1985, just prior to the total U.S. embargo, 20 percent was Nicaraguan. U.S. programming had dropped to 59 percent, and the Socialist countries and the rest of the world were contributing 3 and 18 percent, respectively.[2]

SOCIETY

In social conditions and structures, Nicaragua has much more in common with the rest of Latin America than it does in many aspects of culture. This is not particularly surprising, since most social phenomena are at least partly the product of fairly universal economic and political factors. Nicaragua shares with the other Latin American countries the twin legacies of Iberian colonialism and dependent capitalist "development." Throughout Latin America, the human exploitation and rigid social stratification institutionalized during the colonial era were intensified by the income-concentrating tendencies of modern dependent capitalism.

Demographic Conditions

Like most other Latin American countries, Nicaragua has experienced tremendous demographic change in the twentieth century. Population growth rates have soared, the median age has dropped to around fifteen, and there has been a population shift away from the country toward the urban areas.

The population explosion is a fairly recent phenomenon. True, Nicaragua traditionally has had a very high birth rate. High birth rates seem to be a predictable byproduct of poverty—especially in rural societies. Yet until the mid-twentieth century, the country's fertility was very nearly counterbalanced by the high death rate, resulting in only gradual net gains. In this century, however, major advances in medical science have made it fairly easy throughout the world to significantly reduce death by contagious disease, especially among infants and children. Prodded and assisted by international organizations such as the United Nations, even the most socially insensitive regimes such as the Somoza dictatorship were able to introduce new technologies that significantly reduced the death rate. In the 1950s and 1960s this meant that the Nicaraguan population grew at an annual rate approaching 3 percent. To compound the problem the population was becoming younger and, as a result, even more fertile. This in turn pushed the growth rate in the early 1970s to 3.4 percent annually,[3] which meant that, if nothing changed, the population would double every twenty-one years.

The Somoza regime's response to the population trend was to encourage the people to use birth control devices. A family planning program was created in 1967 that, after about a decade, was operating out of approximately seventy clinics. Even so, it is estimated that only about 5 percent of all women of fertile age used birth control devices.[4]

Nevertheless, though the population growth rate had serious long-range implications, Nicaragua was by no means in imminent danger of a Malthusian disaster. It was still a relatively underpopulated country and, although the War of Liberation had been followed by the inevitable "baby boom," there were at least two factors that could be expected to help moderate growth trends. First, movement away from abject poverty has tended, historically, to reduce fertility. Therefore, assuming that the tremendous energy of the Sandinista Revolution could once again be directed out of defense and back into socially productive projects aimed at raising the standard of living of the people, one could expect the birth rate to drop. Then, too, one could predict that urbanization in Nicaragua would eventually have a moderating effect on fertility as it appears to have had in other Latin American countries such as Colombia, which underwent that phenomenon a decade or so earlier.

Urbanization in Nicaragua, as elsewhere in Latin America, is also a phenomenon of the twentieth century. In 1900, fewer than one in every three Nicaraguans lived in towns and cities of one thousand inhabitants or more. By 1980, however, approximately half were urban dwellers. Since birth rates in the cities are lower than those in the country, the urbanization of Nicaragua appears to have been essentially the product of rural-urban migration. People were leaving the countryside. They were motivated on the one hand by "push" factors such as land concentration, seasonal unemployment, and inhuman rural working conditions. Although the new government began to alleviate these problems by the early 1980s, the activities of the *contras* soon provided another powerful incentive for rural folk to flee to more protected urban areas. On the other hand, the cities exercised a certain "pull" by offering somewhat better health care and educational opportunities and the illusion of a better standard of living.

Urbanization has had some important effects on Nicaragua. In a very real sense, it made possible the Sandinist Revolution. Decades of government corruption and insensitivity in the face of the miserable condition of many poor urban dwellers throughout the country provided a powerful incentive for the urban insurrection. Without mass urban participation, the small FSLN army in the field would surely have had a much more difficult time in defeating the murderous National Guard. Another effect of urbanization—one with which the revolutionary government had to come to grips—is the maldistribution of the work force. During its first years in power the government was faced paradoxically with manpower shortages in some rural areas and massive unemployment in the cities. Its long-range plan for dealing with this problem was to entice movement back to the country by providing better rural health care and educational facilities and fostering more humane living and working conditions.

Social Cleavage

By comparison with many other Latin American societies, Nicaragua is relatively integrated. However, measured against an ideal standard, it still had a long way to go when the Sandinists took power in 1979. The most obvious dimensions of cleavage in Nicaraguan society relate to region, ethnic origin, sex, and class. The first three present less serious problems than the last.

Over the last century the problem of regionalism has become

steadily less important. The relocation of the national capital to Managua in 1852 and several generations of elite intermarriage have reduced the old rivalry between the colonial cities of León and Granada to a triviality. In addition, the construction of highways and railroads in the twentieth century has tended to integrate other formerly remote areas. Perhaps the greatest single problem of regional integration relates to the much neglected Atlantic department of Zelaya, where large segments of the population still look upon the central government with distrust.

The problem of the Atlantic region is also Nicaragua's major ethnic problem. The inhabitants of sparsely populated Zelaya are culturally and racially distinct, and they have a history of separateness that dates to pre-Columbian times. Unlike the original inhabitants of western Nicaragua, who were largely of Meso-American origin, the pre-Columbian peoples of the eastern coast were descendants of immigrants from South America. Later, during the colonial period, when the region fell under the control of the British, English-speaking black slaves were introduced into the region. As a result of these factors, most of the people of the Atlantic region speak English and/ or Indian languages rather than Spanish, are Protestant rather than Catholic, and have a variety of cultural traditions distinct from those of the country's Hispanic majority.

Not surprisingly, the region in which the Sandinist government found the greatest difficulty in implementing its revolutionary programs was the Atlantic coast. This was not for lack of good intentions. Immediately after the liberation, the government affirmed its interest in the welfare of the region. Attractive billboards in Managua enthusiastically proclaimed: "The Atlantic Coast: An Awakening Giant." The Sandinist television network featured Miskito dance groups. Misurasata, an organization of Indians living in that region, was given a seat on the Council of State. The literacy campaign and virtually every government social program had a component designed for the Atlantic coast. Indeed, the new government spent more per capita on social and economic projects for the people of the Atlantic region than for any other part of the country. Nevertheless, although people at the higher levels of government seemed to appreciate the need to treat the country's indigenous minorities with respect and care, soldiers and middle- and lower-level bureaucrats were sometimes quite insensitive and abusive. The ugly incidents that resulted tended to increase the distrust that many *costeños* (coastal people) already felt for the people of western Nicaragua.

The problem had deep historical roots. When the British crown and pirates dominated the coast, local natives allied themselves with those groups against the "Spaniards"—as western Nicaraguans are still known locally. The Somozas used them in disproportionate numbers in the National Guard because of their willingness to fight westerners. Neither Sandino in the 1930s nor the FSLN in the 1970s had much following on the coast. Indeed, many *costeños* still remembered and resented the fact that some of Sandino's guerrilla operations in Zelaya disrupted foreign-owned extractive industries in which they had once been employed.

This historical legacy, coupled with mistakes made early in the period of Sandinista rule, meant that the Atlantic coast was a highly visible Achilles' heel by the time Ronald Reagan came to office in the United States. It appears to have become almost immediately the focal point of CIA-sponsored activity against the Sandinistas. Powerful radio stations beamed scare propaganda into the region. Miskito young people were recruited or pressed into *contra* forces operating out of bases in Honduras. By late 1981, the Nicaraguan government had uncovered "Operation Red Christmas," an alleged CIA plot to separate the Atlantic region from the rest of Nicaragua and thus provide a possible seat for an alternative government.[5] For both humanitarian and security reasons, the Sandinista government soon responded to increased *contra* raids along the Río Coco in northern Zelaya by moving almost 10,000 Indians to safer locations further south. Though conducted in a humane fashion,[6] these moves *were* involuntary, thus further exacerbating Miskito-Sandinista tensions. Over the next year or so the situation worsened. During the ensuing security operations, several hundred indigenous leaders suspected of subversive activities were detained without adequate due process, and as many as 150 individuals either disappeared permanently after being arrested or (as in the case of the massacre at Leimos) were executed outright.[7] Although the persons committing these acts had clearly disobeyed orders (many were later tried and punished), relations with the Atlantic peoples remained very poor until the government late in 1983 began a series of attempts at reconciliation. Starting at that time with an amnesty for Miskito prisoners, the government took a number of steps that, by mid-1985, appeared likely to result in a constitutional arrangement that would give a high degree of autonomy to the indigenous peoples. Nevertheless, a complete resolution of the problem still seemed a long way off.

The problem of integrating the Atlantic coast affects less than 8 percent of the country's population, but the issue of sexism affects over 50 percent. As elsewhere in Latin America, values and ideas connected with the concept of *machismo* (manliness) have traditionally affected sex roles in Nicaragua. Though things were changing, Nicaragua was still very much a man's world in the 1970s. The woman's place was in her home and a strict double standard of sexual behavior applied. On the whole, women received less education and, when employed, earned less money than men. The plight of poor women was especially aggravated by the nature of the Somoza dictatorship and its National Guard. Officers of the guard controlled a flourishing prostitution industry, and soldiers were rarely punished for rape.

Though it would be naive to think that, even in a revolution, sexism could be abolished overnight, it is clear that the national liberation struggle and the revolution greatly advanced the cause of woman's liberation in Nicaragua. The vital part played by women in the War of Liberation caused a healthy reevaluation of sex stereotypes. The Association of Women Confronting the National Problem (AMPRONAC) set up neighborhood committees that helped organize the urban resistance, and many young women fought and died alongside their male counterparts in the FSLN guerrilla army. According to male soldiers with whom I spoke, women—who made up more than 25 percent of the FSLN army—were not camp followers but fully integrated soldiers who shared all of the responsibility of the campaign. They were admired and respected by their male counterparts. The women veterans spoke of warm bonds of respect and love that marked their guerrilla experience.

In postliberation Nicaragua, women continued to play an active and more equal role. They were prominent not only in the new government but also in the Sandinist Popular Army, the Sandinist National Police (which was eventually headed by a woman), and the Sandinist Popular Militias. In addition, AMPRONAC metamorphosed into a Sandinist organization, the Luisa Amanda Espinosa Association of Nicaraguan Women (AMNLAE), which was represented on the Council of State. There they pushed for and frequently won legislation promoting the interests of women.[8]

By far the most serious dimension of social cleavage in Nicaragua is that of class. Before the revolution there was a very wide gap in standard of living between the privileged 20 percent of the population and the impoverished 80 percent. As elsewhere in Latin America, the usual European and North American class categories were inadequate to describe the Nicaraguan class structure. The problem lay in the fact that although the bulk of the privileged class could be described as belonging to a "middle group" or "middle sector" by virtue of occupation and standard of living, they were definitely not a distinct "middle class." Rather than having their own set of values and distinct group identification, members of the middle sector tended to ape and identify with the tiny upper class. The real distinguishing factor in Nicaragua was whether or not one worked with one's hands. Quite simply, 80 percent did and 20 percent did not. Since any physical work was viewed as degrading, the privileged minority was accustomed to hiring lower-class individuals at very low pay to cook their meals, care for their children, clean their homes, tend their yards, shine their shoes, and tote their luggage. This was the "natural" order of things. And whereas *la sociedad*, the people of the upper class or high society, often looked down on members of the middle sector, there was much less distance between the two privileged groups than between them and the impoverished majority.

The distance between the masses and the privileged classes was also maintained symbolically. Titles denoting university degrees—doctor, licenciate, engineer, architect, etc.—were taken very seriously in prerevolutionary Nicaragua. Lower-class individuals were expected to use them with the family name or the respectful *don* or *doña* with the given name in addressing their "superiors." And, whereas the privileged minority were accustomed to employ the familiar *vos* form with their inferiors, the latter were expected to respond with the respectful formal *usted*. This verbal underscoring of class distance even applied in communication between privileged children and their nursemaids. The child was *usted* and the servant, *vos*.

Privileged status was also demonstrated in a number of other ways. Membership in a country club or prestigious social organization, the consumption of imported luxury goods, travel abroad, and the affectation of foreign mannerisms all helped distinguish *gente decente* ("decent people") from the masses.

Although the overthrow of the Somozas was a product of the combined efforts of all classes, it was inevitable that, if it were to be a real revolution with meaningful change, there would be class tension and conflict after the liberation. By definition, social revolution involves a reordering of the relationship between classes. Former privileged groups are asked—or obliged—to make sacrifices so that the nation's limited resources can be redirected into the human development of the majority.

In the case of Nicaragua, the revolution affected the former privileged classes negatively in a number of ways. The use of *don* or *doña*, or of university titles, became less common. *Compañero* or its more common variants, *compa* or *compita*, became the usual form of address, at least among revolutionaries. Country clubs were confiscated and put to other uses including recreation for the public. The importation of luxury goods was curtailed. Many rural and urban properties were seized, and stiff taxes were levied on property, income, and domestic luxury items such as cigarettes and rum.

Many Nicaraguans understood and were able to accommodate themselves to this new reality. The relatively privileged parents of the tens of thousands of high school and college students who participated in the Literacy Crusade of 1980, for instance, demonstrated their willingness to cooperate with the revolution by giving their children the required permission to join the crusade. Many businessmen and landholders responded to government pleas to reactivate the economy by returning their properties to normal production.

But many members of the former privileged classes were a good bit less generous and understanding. Some simply liquidated their assets and fled the country, joining more than ten thousand Somoza followers already exiled in northern Central America and the United States. Others stayed on, grumbling and resisting. Within days of the liberation, for instance, I was asked by a lawyer friend to help get his teenaged children into an English language program in the United States so they, in his words, would not "waste" the months that school would be out during the literacy campaign. Bitter jokes about the revolution and its leaders became standard fare at some gatherings. Rumors of all sorts spread like wildfire in privileged circles (one even claimed that the immediate postwar shortage of beans and medicine was due to the fact that these precious materials were being diverted to Cuba).

More seriously, fearing that Nicaragua was becoming "another Cuba," many landholders and businessmen refused to cooperate in the reconstruction. They began decapitalizing their properties instead of reinvesting in spite of repeated assurances that a responsible private sector would be preserved along with very generous government loans, tax incentives, and concessionary rates of currency exchange.

As we noted earlier, bourgeois resistance began almost immediately after the Triumph. Several recently founded or reorganized microparties began issuing shrill statements reflecting the fears of the privileged classes. In May of 1980, *La Prensa* took a sharp political jag to the right. At the same time, several tiny counterrevolutionary "armies"—such as the so-called Democratic Armed Forces (FAD), which had been organized by disgruntled cattlemen—began harassing the government. Though posing no real threat to the regime, these "armies" and former National Guardsmen operating out of safe sanctuary in Honduras did manage to inflict property damage and take innocent lives, including those of seven young literacy campaigners.

The position of the privileged classes hardened even more after the election of Ronald Reagan in the United States in November

A cartoon commentary on the attitude of the privileged classes (as represented by the figure in the derby hat). (Courtesy of *Cartoons from Nicaragua: The Revolutionary Humor of Roger* [Managua: Committee of U.S. Citizens Living in Nicaragua, 1984])

1980. At that point, paramilitary activities increased and the church hierarchy, La Prensa, the opposition microparties, and the Superior Council of Private Enterprise (COSEP) closed ranks in a more concerted effort to reverse history. Although their activities were couched in terms of the defense of "freedom of the press," and of the preservation of "religious liberty" and a "mixed economy," those were not the issues. Neither of the latter two had been threatened at all and press freedom was severely limited only in 1982, almost three years after the Triumph, when the country was clearly under internationally organized paramilitary attack. In reality, the heart of the matter was power. The church hierarchy feared an erosion of religious control and authority in the face of the immense popularity of the revolution and the new process of democratization within the church that had begun at Medellín. The privileged classes in general sensed, quite accurately, that they had lost political power. The Sandinistas had been quite willing to allow these groups political participation at least equivalent to the percentage they represented within the population. But that was not enough. As long as the expectation remained that the contras or the U.S. Marines might someday deliver power back into their hands, there would be no incentive to adjust to the new system. Accordingly, of all the internal problems faced by the revolution, that of class was clearly the most serious.

REVOLUTIONARY SOCIAL PROGRAMS

The most important long-term concern of the Sandinist Revolution was to improve the human condition of the downtrodden majority of the Nicaraguan people. From its founding in 1961 to its final triumph in 1979, the FSLN repeatedly advocated a variety of sweeping social reforms. Immediately after their entry into Managua, therefore, the revolutionaries began to put promises into effect. Ironically, their efforts were made very difficult by the terrible domestic economic situation and the huge international debt inherited from the departing dictator and his cronies. The government had very little in public revenues with which to finance social programs and was forced to ask the working classes to show restraint in making admittedly justifiable wage demands—especially in the public sector.

In spite of these problems, the revolutionaries made impressive progress in the social area during their first six years in power. Almost immediately after their victory, in order to combat unemployment in urban areas, they embarked on a variety of labor-intensive public works projects financed out of a special Fund to Combat Unemployment. The revenues for this fund were raised through a tax on the "thirteenth month" salary that all employers were obliged to pay their employees at Christmas. The privileged minority of wage earners entitled to more than $150 (U.S.) in their extra month's salary were required to forgo that part of their bonus in order that thousands of their less fortunate countrymen be employed. The middle sector complained bitterly, but this fund and other monies—some from international sources—allowed the government not only to provide jobs but also to engage in public works projects designed to improve the lives of the people. These included a fifty-square-block children's park in the heart of old Managua, public dance and assembly facilities, several clean and well-constructed public marketplaces, simple and hygienic concession stands, covered picnic areas, sidewalks, paved roads in poor neighborhoods, and the reconstruction of war-damaged roads in urban areas.

The new government was also concerned with improving the lives of the rural poor. Immediately after the liberation, the government confiscated the agrarian properties of Somoza and his cohorts—about one-fifth of the nation's cultivable land. During the following years additional confiscations took place for other reasons, so that, by 1984, large private landholdings, which had represented 52 percent of total farmland in 1978, had been reduced to 26 percent. Although some of the land confiscated had been distributed to individual peasants, the major beneficiaries of this change were peasant cooperatives and state farms; they had not even existed in 1978, but now they controlled 36 and 19 percent of the land, respectively.[9] (Significantly, by the mid-1980s there was a clear trend away from state farms toward private cooperative forms of land utilization. The latter were more productive and more conducive to the overall political objective of creating a participatory citizen.) On the state farms and cooperatives, efforts were made to improve the lives of the rural poor by upgrading working conditions; providing small health units, schools, housing projects, and day-care centers; and opening rural stores in which the prices for basic necessities were kept artificially low.

In the segment of private agriculture that had not been organized into cooperatives, the government worked in behalf of the poor in a number of additional ways. To help the agricultural proletariat working on large private farms, it began strict enforcement of laws governing minimum wages and working conditions and encouraged workers, through their unions, to insist on their rights. In addition, for the first time in history, small producers were given access to substantial amounts of public credit. In the first year over 50 percent of all public loans to the agrarian private sector went to credit and service cooperatives formed by peasants. Later a program was begun that gave titles of ownership to large numbers of peasants who had previously occupied and used land without legal guarantees. Small farmers were also helped by strict controls governing water usage and maximum rents for agricultural lands.[10]

In spite of severe economic constraints, the government also implemented sweeping changes in public policy toward health, social security, food, housing, and education.[11] Efforts in the area of health were impressive. Even during the insurrection, the FSLN, through its neighborhood Civil Defense Committees (CDCs), had organized health volunteers to deal with the most pressing medical needs of people in the insurgent neighborhoods. Immediately after the liberation, the poorly coordinated, chaotic, clientelistic health care system inherited from Somoza was thoroughly reorganized into one administratively centralized ministry. The overriding philosophy of the new system was to make health care available to everyone in rural and urban areas alike.

A major dilemma for the Sandinistas in these years was to decide whether, on the one hand, to emphasize expensive curative health care (hospitals, doctors, etc.) or, on the other, to opt for more effective but also less politically glamorous preventative programs. In the long run, the government ended up doing both. Government expenditures in the area of health increased over 200 percent from 1978 to 1983. The most costly aspect of the program related to the rebuilding, expansion, and staffing of curative facilities such as hospitals and clinics. At the same time heavy emphasis was also placed on primary or preventative health care, and in 1981 the United Nations Children's Fund (UNICEF) chose Nicaragua as a demonstration site for this type of approach to health. Here, voluntary labor was crucial. Within months of the Sandinista victory, inoculation campaigns had been carried out, at low cost, by mass organizations. By 1982, over seventy-eight thousand volunteer health *brigadistas* had been mobilized to work in a variety of preventative projects on designated Popular Health Days (Jornadas Populares de Salud). As a result of these efforts, not a single confirmed case of polio occurred in 1982, and by 1983 infant diarrhea, mountain leprosy, and malaria were down 75, 60, and 50 percent, respectively. Infant mortality in general was down from 121 per thousand in 1978 and 1979 to 90.1 per thousand in 1983. Life expectancy had crept up from 52.2 to 57.6 years.

Early on, the social security and social welfare functions of the government were reorganized, separated from those having to do with health, and consolidated into one institution—the Nicaraguan Social Security and Welfare Institute (INSSBI). The latter not only extended social security coverage to a wider segment of society but also took on the responsibility of dealing with problems related to social welfare such as the rehabilitation of prostitutes and delinquent minors, the care of orphans, the creation of day-care centers, the building and administration of workers' recreation facilities, and so on. Eventually, it was also put in charge of handling the emergency needs of displaced persons—first the victims of the 1982 flood and later the more than 180,000 persons made homeless by the CIA-coordinated *contra* war.

The revolution also brought an abrupt change in government policy regarding food. Under the Somozas, the majority of Nicaraguans had suffered from malnutrition. Much of the country's best lands had been used to produce agro-export products for the benefit of the few. Domestic food production was inadequate. Much food was imported. Prices were high. The Sandinistas, however, immediately placed a high priority on making basic staples available to all at reasonable prices. The tactics employed were complex. Farmers were given incentives to increase the production of staples while, at the same time, the state played a prominent role in the storage, distribution, and pricing of basic foods through its new state-owned food marketing enterprise (ENABAS). Because demand shot up and importations went down before production in all areas reached a sufficient level, the government also found it necessary to institute a system of rationing of certain basic staples so that all people could have relatively equal access to those items regardless of class. But there were problems: Middle- and upper-class people grumbled about scarcity in super-markets (most Nicaraguans shop in people's stores and public markets), ration cards, standing in line, and so forth. Market people were upset that they had fewer imported products to sell and that consumer prices in people's stores were artificially low. But by 1983, the program was showing results. Although the per capita intake of corn had remained stagnant over 1977 levels and that for beans had increased only slightly, the consumption of rice was up 66 percent. In addition, although the consumption of beef and milk were down 10 and 4 percent, respectively, the intake of eggs, cooking oil, and poultry were up 21, 30, and 80 percent, respectively.[12]

The new government was also concerned with helping the people secure what the Sandinists viewed as the basic human right to shelter. As in the area of other social services, the devastation caused by the war accentuated an already bleak situation in housing. The basic philosophy of the new Ministry of Housing and Human Settlements (MINVAH) was both humanitarian and practical. In the practical sense, aware of the inadequacy, waste, and high cost of public housing programs in capitalist and socialist countries alike, the revolutionaries decided not to embark on a massive government program of housing construction. Some government housing was constructed—especially in connection with agricultural production centers. But the major thrust of new Sandinist policy was to provide legal protection to the renter and homeowner and to supply infrastructural, technical, and organizational support for the construction of new housing. Accordingly, drastic rent reduction and controls were immediately implemented. Illegal subdivisions, in which wealthy landowners had been selling small building plots on the installment plan without supplying basic services, were nationalized. The government also moved to outlaw urban land speculation and passed legislation that allowed it to confiscate unused lands needed for housing projects. In 1981, it began implementing a "sites and services" approach to housing. In projects called "progressive urbanizations," which markedly increased in number following the population dislocations caused by the 1982 floods, the homeless were given title to plots and provided with basic utilities and services, but were left on their own to improve their dwellings and create their own organizations to solve community problems.

Clearly the greatest strides in social reform in these years were made in the area of education. The first and most dramatic event in this respect was the National Literacy Crusade of 1980. From March to August of that year all schools were closed as over sixty thousand young volunteers dispersed throughout the country while another twenty-five thousand worked in the cities in an attempt to bring literacy to the majority of the population over ten years old who could neither read nor write. According to official results the illiteracy rate for persons ten years old and older was reduced in those five months from over 50 percent to less than 13 percent. Though many people hostile to the revolution claimed that the Sandinists had greatly exaggerated their achievement, a fair examination of methods, tactics, and resources reveals that gains in the general neighborhood of those claimed by the government were at least plausible.

A literacy campaign of the type carried out by Nicaragua in 1980 would have been impossible in most of the prerevolutionary societies of Latin America. Prohibitively expensive in an unmobilized society, such a campaign would also have amounted to an administrative and logistical nightmare of the first magnitude. For the highly mobilized society of postliberation Nicaragua, however, this crusade was neither inordinately expensive nor exceptionally difficult to coordinate and implement. The key to its success was the voluntary participation not only of the young teachers and their previously illiterate students but also of various Sandinist popular organizations (described in Chapter 6), which provided free and vitally important logistical support. Their efforts were also backed by a substantial segment of the Catholic Church, the private sector, and various other organizations. Under such circumstances, the government's major function was simply to plan the campaign, train the literacy volunteers, and provide some material assistance. Given a target illiterate population (ten years or over) of under eight hundred thousand, the student-teacher ratio was very favorable and the time involved was sufficient to teach basic reading and writing skills.[13]

The idea of a literacy crusade had been gestating for some time. The FSLN—and in particular one of its martyred founders, Carlos Fonseca Amador—had often stressed the need for such a campaign. Planning sessions had taken place before the final FSLN victory. After the liberation, Nicaragua's new leaders forged ahead with this ambitious project in spite of dire warnings by learned international authorities that their effort was premature and destined to fail.

The Nicaraguans were blessed in that they could draw selectively upon the experience of several mass literacy campaigns attempted previously in other parts of the world. In the 1920s, the Mexican Revolution made a primitive attempt at a literacy campaign. In mid-century, Paulo Freire developed a methodology that he first attempted to apply in his native Brazil and then, after the military coup of 1964, took with greater success to other Third World countries, including Guinea-Bissau in the mid-1970s. In 1961, Cuba carried out its revolutionary literacy campaign. Not surprisingly, therefore, the Nicaraguan crusade received the enthusiastic assistance of many international experts. Paulo Freire himself was an adviser to the crusade's national coordinating body, Cuba sent advisers, the United Nations Economic and Social Council (ECOSOC) supplied verbal support and technical advice, and many individuals, including some U.S. citizens, volunteered.

The crusade was planned in stages. Soon after the liberation, the popular organizations (CDS, AMNLAE, etc.) conducted a surprisingly thorough and sophisticated nationwide census to determine the characteristics and problems of the Nicaraguan people, especially in the area of literacy. At the same time a team of literacy experts worked to prepare a twenty-three lesson literacy primer. The crusade took place in concentric waves. First eighty selected educators took a fifteen-day seminar in literacy training. After testing what they had learned in the field, each member taught another group; then they and the members of the second group taught hundreds of additional educators, bringing the total of literacy trainers to several thousand.

The 1980 Literacy Crusade. In March, 60,000 volunteer teachers departed for rural areas (*top*) while 25,000 stayed in the cities, teaching at night in such unlikely locations as the onion stall of a public market (*bottom*). Though the initial and most ambitious phase of the crusade was completed and commemorated with a celebration in August (*top*), other

aspects of this program such as follow-up education for the newly literate and literacy education in English and Miskito (*bottom*) demonstrated the new government's ongoing concern for basic popular education. (Photos courtesy of Ramón Zamora Olivas of the central office of the National Literacy Crusade)

At that point all of the trainers were dispersed to various regions of the country to teach the volunteers. Finally, from March to August 1980, the volunteers themselves fanned out across the land to teach the illiterates who had been identified by the census.

In 1980, the Year of Literacy, the crusade became the focus of national attention. The imagery employed flowed out of the War of Liberation of the previous year. This second war of liberation was designed not only to free the masses from ignorance and intellectual subjugation, but, equally important, to liberate the largely middle-class volunteers themselves from their prejudices and stereotypes about Nicaragua's impoverished majority. The country was broken into "fronts" corresponding to the six zones of combat during the liberation struggle. Within each front, there were literacy "columns," "squadrons," and individual *brigadistas* (brigadiers). In many cases the *brigadistas* lived and worked during the day with the peasants and workers whom they taught at night.

From the start, the teaching of "political literacy" was also very much a part of the campaign. Paulo Freire's concept of *concientização* ("consciousness-raising") was essential. Key words, phrases, and sentences in each of the lessons were designed to stimulate discussion and a new patriotism, pride in the revolution and its martyrs, and, especially, a sense of the dignity and importance of the individual. The first lesson, for instance, focused on *la revolución*, words of central political importance that, at the same time, contained all of the basic vowels. Predictably, many members of the privileged classes, as well as a number of foreign observers, saw the campaign as little more than a systematic program of Marxist or Communist indoctrinations. However, there was nothing in the primer or the teachers manual, or in any of the other teaching aids used, that would justify that charge. There *was* a political message. But it was nationalist and revolutionary, somewhat analogous to the message young people in the United States receive when they learn about the American Revolution in grade school. Interestingly, the director of the crusade was a Jesuit priest, Father Fernando Cardenal.

In the end, the key to the success of the crusade lay in massive voluntary participation. No one was forced to participate. Indeed, minors were not allowed to join without the permission of their parents. Yet for five months the streets of Managua and other major cities were strangely quiet as a significant segment of the country's urban teenagers and young adults waged Nicaragua's second war of liberation in the countryside. In all, this participation, the logistical support of the church and the Sandinist popular organizations, and money and materials from all over the world ultimately made it possible for the government to coordinate a massive project at a small cost to itself.

The literacy crusade, which won for Nicaragua the 1980 award of the United Nations Educational, Scientific, and Cultural Organization (UNESCO) for the best program of its kind, was not intended as a one-shot affair. It was followed later in that year by literacy crusades in Miskito and English for the peoples of the Atlantic region and by the beginning of a massive adult education program aimed at eventually lifting all Nicaraguans to the equivalency of a minimum of four years of schooling. By 1982, total enrollment at all levels of education was approximately twice what it had been in 1978. And in 1983, Nicaragua was claiming an illiteracy rate of only 10 percent— one of the lowest in Latin America.

In all, the Sandinista Revolution in its first six years had embarked on an ambitious and multifaceted program of social change. By 1983, these programs were registering impressive results. Even the Kissinger Commission Report, published in January of the following year, admitted grudgingly that "Nicaragua's government has made significant gains against illiteracy and disease."[14] Ironically, by 1984 and 1985, the various advances made in the first four years were slowly but surely being reversed. The *contras* were routinely attacking and destroying social service infrastructure and personnel; over 40 percent of the budget was being diverted to national defense; and the government program in food price subsidies was dropped and other programs in health, housing, education, and social welfare, though continued on a reduced scale, were palpably affected.

NOTES

1. For a review of Chamorro's works and exact bibliographical citation see either Grafton Conliffe and Thomas W. Walker, "The Crucified Nicaragua of Pedro Joaquín Chamorro," *Latin American Research Review*, vol. 13, no. 3 (Fall 1978), pp. 183–188; or Grafton Conliffe and Thomas W. Walker, "The Literary Works of Pedro Joaquín Chamorro," *Caribbean Review*, vol. 7, no. 4 (October-December 1978), pp. 46–50.

2. Interview with Oscar Miranda, Sandinista TV System (SSTV), June 20, 1985.

3. United Nations, *1978 Statistical Yearbook* (New York: United Nations Publishing, 1979), p. 70.

4. An anonymous informed source.

5. "Nicaragua: Sandinista Accusations of Reagan Destabilization," *Central America Report* (March 6, 1982), p. 70.

6. Amnesty International, for instance, stated outright that "reports of shootings of civilians and other deliberate brutality during the transfer were

later shown to be false, and government medical and other civilian personnel assisted residents during the transfer." See Amnesty International, "Nicaragua Background Briefing: Persistence of Public Order Law Detentions and Trials" (London, 1982), p. 8. Ironically, the Reagan administration had painted quite a different picture, accusing the Sandinistas of wholesale human rights violations equivalent to those perpetrated by the Nazis during the Second World War. For a discussion of how the Reagan administration misinformed the public on this issue, see Thomas W. Walker, "Nicaraguan-U.S. Friction: The First Four Years, 1979–1983," in Kenneth M. Coleman and George G. Herring, *The Central American Crisis: Sources of Conflict and the Failure of U.S. Policy* (Wilmington, Del.: Scholarly Resources, 1985), pp. 183–184.

7. For a lengthy examination of this matter see Inter-American Commission on Human Rights, Organization of American States, *Report on the Situation of Human Rights of a Segment of the Nicaraguan Population of Miskito Origin* (Washington, D.C.: OAS, 1984).

8. For a discussion of the role of women in revolutionary Nicaragua see Maxine Molyneux, "Women," in Thomas W. Walker, ed., *Nicaragua: The First Five Years* (New York: Praeger Publishers, 1985), pp. 145–162.

9. Jaime Wheelock Román, *Entre la crisis y la agresión: la Reforma Agraria Sandinista* (Managua: Editorial Nueva Nicaragua, 1985), p. 119.

10. For more details about agrarian reform in Nicaragua see Joseph R. Thome and David Kaimowitz, "Agrarian Reform," in Walker, ed., *Nicaragua: The First Five Years*, pp. 299–316.

11. For more information about these major social programs see (1) Deborah Barndt, "Popular Education," (2) Thomas John Bossert, "Health Policy: The Dilemma of Success," (3) Reinaldo Antonio Téfel et al., "Social Welfare," (4) Harvey Williams, "Housing Policy," and (5) James E. Austin and Jonathan Fox, "Food Policy," in Walker, ed., *Nicaragua: The First Five Years*, pp. 347–422.

12. These statistics are from Austin and Fox, "Food Policy," p. 409. For an excellent book on food policy in Nicaragua see Joseph Collins, *Nicaragua: What Difference Could a Revolution Make? Food and Farming in the New Nicaragua*, 2d ed. (San Francisco: Institute for Food and Development Policy, 1985).

13. Previously illiterate individuals were ultimately reclassified as literate if they were able to pass a basic reading and writing test upon successfully completing all twenty-three lessons in the literacy primer.

14. Kissinger Commission, *Report of the National Bipartisan Commission on Central America* (Washington, D.C.: U.S. Government Printing Office, 1984), p. 30.

6
Government and Politics

A political system is not simply a matter of electoral procedures, constitutions, and governmental structures. Politics also involves the relationship between groups and classes and all other factors that impinge on the character of governmental output. For this reason, a narrow examination of the formal constitutional and structural characteristics of a government—especially in the Third World context—is frequently not only misleading but also essentially an empty intellectual exercise. This is certainly true for Nicaragua, particularly in the period before the FSLN victory in 1979.

THE PREREVOLUTIONARY SYSTEM

If one had been foolish enough to take seriously the constitutional formalities and stated objectives of the Nicaraguan government during the Somoza years, one would surely have come to the mistaken conclusion that Nicaragua was blessed with a modern democratic form of government that was pursuing praiseworthy developmental goals. According to the constitution, there were free elections, separation of powers, and a full gamut of explicitly guaranteed human rights. To insure minority participation, the major opposition party was automatically awarded 40 percent of all seats in the legislature and minority representation on boards of government agencies, judgeships, etc. What is more, there were a variety of public agencies and institutions such as the Central Bank, the National Development Institute, the Nicaraguan Agrarian Institute, the Institute of Internal-External Commerce, and the Social Security Institute, which were ostensibly designed to cope with the problems faced by a modernizing society. The stated policies of the government were also impressive. The major expressed goal was to develop the country through the modernization and diversification of the economy. Accordingly, highly trained technocrats were given important roles in the development process and lofty five-year plans were issued and subsequently endorsed by lists of international agencies.

All of this, of course, was simply a facade. Government and politics, under the Somozas, were "of, by, and for" the privileged few. Democracy was nonexistent, corruption was elaborately institutionalized, and public policy consistently ignored the well-being of the majority of the population.

Nicaragua was a democracy in name only. Although there were constitutional provisions for the separation of power—with a bicameral legislature, an executive, and a judiciary—in reality, all power was concentrated in the hands of the president. The National Guard was the president's private army. His command over the Liberal party—which in turn dominated both houses of the legislature and all government agencies—meant that the president was, in fact, the only decision maker. Mandated minority participation served only to legitimize the system and to co-opt Conservative politicians. There was never any possibility that the opposition would come to power legally since elections were thoroughly rigged. During campaign periods, there was frequent censorship of the press and intimidation of opposition candidates. On election day, there was multiple voting by the pro-Somoza faithful, tampering with the ballot boxes, and, cleverest of all, the use of a translucent "secret" ballot that, even when folded, could easily be scrutinized by government election officials as it was deposited in the ballot box.

Given the hopelessly undemocratic character of elections under the Somozas, party organization and activity were shallow and essentially without meaning. The two major parties, Liberal and Conservative, were crusty relics of the nineteenth century. The original ideological differences between them had long since faded into insignificance. Both represented the interests of a small privileged minority and, by the middle of the twentieth century, both had been co-opted and emasculated by the Somoza system.

Officially, the Somozas were Liberals and their governments were Liberal administrations. In fact, however, throughout most of the period, the Liberal party was simply a cosmetic appendage to a system that depended on brute military force. One apparent exception occurred in the late 1950s and early 1960s when Luis Somoza—who enjoyed the trappings of democracy and party politics—encouraged the Liberal party to have a life of its own. In that period, new Liberal leaders emerged and there was some hope that they might turn into real presidential prospects. In the late 1960s, after the "election" of the less politically minded Anastasio Somoza Debayle, these hopes were quickly dashed. Independent upstarts left or were drummed out of the party as the dictator began to maneuver to perpetuate himself in power, and the Liberal party lapsed into its more traditional cosmetic role.

The official Conservative opposition played an even less dignified role. If the Liberal party was the neglected wife of the Somoza system, the Conservative party was its kept woman. Since the facade of democracy was so important to the Somozas, it was imperative that there always be an opposition to run against during elections. Enticed by personal bribes and/or lucrative opportunities inherent in mandated minority participation in congress, the judiciary, and government agencies, the leaders of the Conservative party frequently agreed to provide a legitimizing opposition during the rigged elections. Even on those infrequent occasions when the leaders of the Conservative party mustered the dignity to refuse to participate, the dictators were usually able to convince less important Conservatives to carry that party's banner to defeat.

There were a number of microparties during the Somoza period. A few of the more notable were the Independent Liberal party (PLI), composed of Liberals who, from 1944 on, chose to dissociate themselves from the parent party over the issue of Somoza's continuing dominance; the Nicaraguan Social Christian party (PSCN), formed by young Catholic intellectuals in 1957; and the Nicaraguan Socialist party (PSN), which was founded by local Communists in 1944.

One of the more interesting of the microparties was the Social Christian party.[1] Inspired by progressive papal encyclicals, lay Catholic humanism, and Christian Democratic ideas emanating from Europe, this party attempted to take advantage of Luis Somoza's somewhat more open attitude toward competitive political activity. Stressing the importance of platform, ideology, organization, and tactics, the Christian Democrats not only won a significant popular following, but also penetrated the labor movement and came for a while to dominate the national students' organizations. Though many young Christian Democrats freely admitted their admiration for the courage and audacity of FSLN guerrillas, they felt at that time that a peaceful, democratic solution might still be possible. When it became clear in the early 1970s that they were wrong, the more progressive members of the party split from the PSCN to form the Popular Social Christian party (PPSC), which espoused an increasingly revolutionary position.

Mass-interest articulation through legal channels was also a fairly hopeless activity under the Somozas. Peasants and urban labor, for instance, had almost no input into the political system. Ignorant, illiterate, and geographically scattered, the peasantry and rural proletariat were subject to constant abuse by landowners and the National Guard. An agrarian reform program legislated in the early days of the Alliance for Progress had virtually no impact on the misery of the rural poor. From 1964 on, a private Social Christian–oriented organization—the Institute for Human Promotion (INPRHU)—did struggle to organize and raise the consciousness of the peasants, but in the face of government roadblocks, its efforts were largely ineffectual. In the end, clandestine activity proved to be the only viable alternative. In the late 1970s, the FSLN began organizing rural workers and landless peasants in workers' committees. In 1978, these were fused into a national organization—the Rural Workers' Association (ATC). In the following year, as the War of Liberation neared its successful conclusion, ATC-organized peasants made their contribution by digging trenches and felling huge trees across roadways to block troop movements and by maximizing the first post-Somoza harvest through the seizure and immediate cultivation of *Somocista*-owned lands in the newly liberated areas.

The urban worker was only slightly better off than his country cousin. The organized labor movement encompassed a small minority of all workers and was badly fragmented. In 1977, the major union organizations included the Marxist Independent General Confederation of Labor, with 12,000 members; the government-patronized General Confederation of Labor, with 8,000 to 10,000 members; the AFL-CIO-oriented Confederation of Labor Unity, with 7,000 members; and the Social Christian Confederation of Workers of Nicaragua, with 3,000 members. The right to strike, while formally enshrined in law, was so severely restricted that most of the many strikes that took place in the 1960s and 1970s were declared illegal. Collective bargaining was made all but impossible by Article 17 of the *Regulations of Syndical Associations*, which allowed the employer to fire, without explanation, any two leaders of the striking union. In the long run, the only viable option for urban workers, too, was to organize themselves clandestinely—again under FSLN leadership. Significantly, the urban insurrections—which took place almost exclusively in working-class neighborhoods—turned out to be one of the most important ingredients in the overthrow of the dictatorship.

Not surprisingly, given the nearly complete absence of institutionalized popular input into the political system, the Somoza government was virtually oblivious to the interests of the ordinary Nicaraguan citizen. Lofty-sounding social programs—ostensibly concerned with public health, agrarian reform, low-income housing, education, social security, and the like—served mainly as devices to legitimize the system, attract foreign aid, employ the politically faithful, and diversify opportunities for the pilfering of public revenues. Very little of what the government spent actually trickled down to the people. With members of Somoza's family at the head of most government agencies, a large chunk of each agency's assets went directly to satisfy the family's greed. For instance, in the ten years in which he headed the National Institute of Light and Energy, Anastasio Somoza Debayle's uncle, Luis Manuel Debayle, allegedly siphoned off more than $30 million (U.S.). Under the Somozas were layer upon layer of corrupt bureaucrats who were expected and, indeed, encouraged to help themselves. Honesty, a threat to the system, was discouraged.

Often a legalistic patina was applied to these misuses of public revenues. But the end result was that when the FSLN seized power in 1979, it had to cope with acute problems in health, education, housing, and welfare. To add insult to injury, the departing dictator and his accomplices, who had left barely $3 million (U.S.) in the public coffers, had saddled the new government with a whopping $1.6 billion (U.S.) foreign debt.[2]

Whispering greed: During a Somocista gala, Anastasio Somoza Debayle (right) shares a confidence with his uncle, Luis "Tio Luz" Manuel Debayle who, during his ten years as head of the national energy agency, is alleged to have misappropriated in excess of US$30 million. (Photographer unknown)

THE GOVERNMENT OF NATIONAL RECONSTRUCTION

If the old political system had been "of, by, and for" a tiny privileged elite, the revolutionary system that replaced it was clearly based in and oriented toward the interests of the impoverished majority. Whereas democracy under the Somozas meant rigged elections, the empty rhetoric of corrupt elite-oriented parties, and the suppression of popular political participation, the new political system not only involved, but actually depended upon, the mobilization and voluntary participation of hundreds of thousands of ordinary citizens. Not surprisingly, this seismic change in the orientation of politics and government in favor of the "have-nots" was alarming to the former "haves."

The governmental system of revolutionary Nicaragua came into existence gradually over a period of years. Its informal but central element was the nine-person Sandinista Directorate (DN) drawn equally from the three former factions of the FSLN. Until an elected government was inaugurated in January of 1985, each branch of the formal government, though by no means powerless, existed at the pleasure of the DN, which had created it in the first place. The Directorate in turn drew its strength from the legitimacy it had acquired through its leading role in the revolutionary victory, its control of the revolutionary armed forces, and the support of hundreds of thousands of civilians who made up the grassroots organizations that had developed during the insurrection. Within the DN, as earlier noted, decision making was based on consensus or near-consensus; as of mid-1985, open factional disputes had been completely avoided, and none of the nine *comandantes* of 1979 had either resigned or been replaced.

Nevertheless, in spite of its virtually unassailable political advantage, the FSLN chose, for practical reasons, to create a formal governmental structure that would encourage the participation not just of Sandinistas but of almost all other sectors in society as well. This decision was important since the new government needed the cooperation of a variety of groups. The Sandinistas knew that if they were going to preserve a mixed economy with a major role for the private sector, they would have to institutionalize participation by the various parties and interest groups associated with former privileged classes. They had no intention of allowing these minority groups enough political power to deflect or water down their revolution, but they did sincerely want to give them involvement in the system at least equivalent to their numerical weight in the population as a whole. Accordingly, all of the institutions that were created—the

The FSLN Directorate. From left to right: Luis Carrión, Victor Tirado López, Carlos Nuñez, Humberto Ortega Saavedra, Tomás Borge, Bayardo Arce, Jaime Wheelock, Henry Ruíz, and Daniel Ortega Saavedra. (Photo courtesy of *Barricada*)

plural executive, the corporatively organized legislative branch, the ministries, and the judiciary—included non-Sandinistas as well as Sandinistas.

The executive branch originally consisted of a five-person Junta of the Government of National Reconstruction (JGRN) containing two Conservatives, one pro-Sandinista intellectual, and two FSLN guerrilla veterans. Eventually, through resignation and reassignment, the JGRN was reduced to one Conservative and two Sandinistas. Junta member Daniel Ortega—also a member of the Sandinista Directorate—eventually became its head. All of the ministries except interior and defense were placed under the JGRN.

The legislative body, or Council of State, which was formally inaugurated in May of 1980, employed a quasi-corporative system of representation. Virtually all political parties (with the exception of the Somoza branch of the Liberal party) and major pro- and anti-Sandinista interest organizations were assigned seats. Each grouping elected or appointed its own representatives. The size and composition of the council changed over time. Originally envisioned as having thirty-three members, it actually comprised forty-seven when inaugurated in 1980. The Council was eventually expanded to fifty-one before it was superseded by the elected National (Constituent) Assembly in January 1985. These increases reflected the emergence of new interest organizations and parties and the rise or decline of old ones. The traditional parties and interest organizations complained, with accuracy, that pro-Sandinista organizations were given a majority of seats. The Sandinistas responded by indicating, with equal accuracy, that the traditional parties and organizations were actually overrepresented given the small percentage of the population made up of the classes for which they stood.

Changes also occurred in the functions of the Council. Instead of being limited, as originally proposed, to the approval or disapproval of Junta decisions without modifications, the Council had the right to initiate and/or modify legislation. In the words of its first president, Commander Bayardo Arce, it had acquired a "colegislative" function.[3] It is interesting to note that, whereas in 1980-1981 the Junta initiated most bills before the Council (fifty-six as opposed to thirty-nine), the Council itself initiated the majority of bills in the 1982-1983 session (forty-four as opposed to sixteen).[4]

The judicial branch, in its turn, was composed of both regular courts and special tribunals. The regular court system was similar to that of other Latin American countries with *habeas corpus* and various levels of appeal. The members of these courts were lawyers coming from a variety of political backgrounds. Convictions were often overturned on appeal.

The more controversial special tribunals were set up to deal with emergency overloads of the judicial system. These tribunals were created immediately after the victory to try the thousands of National Guardsmen and Somocistas taken prisoner as the old system collapsed. As in the Nuremberg trials following the Second World War, there was an element of *ex post facto* justice. Nevertheless, no official executions occurred, the death penalty was abolished, and the maximum sentence was thirty years. Further, those individuals sentenced on the questionable charge of "illicit association" (for instance, being a member of the National Guard) were duly released when their three-year terms were up. Later, in April 1983, another type of tribunal, the "Popular Anti-Somocista Tribunals" (TPAs), was created to try cases related to the *contra* war and suspected internal counterrevolutionary activity. The TPAs were criticized for not providing sufficient due process. Among other problems, although an appeals process was included within the tribunal system, there was no right to appeal through the regular judicial system.[5] On the other hand, to view this matter in perspective, we should note that *most* governments violate due process during times of national danger. Even Great Britain, normally considered one of the world's greatest democracies, has for decades routinely imposed prolonged imprisonment without trial in the case of suspected members of the Irish Republican Army.

The Sandinistas also moved to decentralize government and administration. At the time of the Triumph, a network of local governments known as Municipal Juntas for Reconstruction (JMRs) were elected in public assemblies. These three- or five-person bodies had the responsibility of coordinating local reconstruction efforts in cooperation with local grassroots organizations and with the departmental and national governments. However, the local governments, lacking authority and resources, found themselves heavily dependent on central government bureaucrats who often had little understanding of local problems. Negative feedback ultimately led the revolutionary government to draft a plan for regionalization and decentralization that was formally inaugurated on July 19, 1982. The country was now divided into six regions and three special zones, each of which had the authority to deal with all government functions. These nine entities were created in accordance with the differing demographic and economic characteristics of different parts of the country. Now local officials, instead of having to deal with an overloaded central bureaucracy, could coordinate their activities directly with regional officials familiar with the needs, problems, and assets of the region.

GROUPS AND POWER

The conduct of government in the first six years was made easier, less expensive, and more responsive to the people by the existence of a variety of volunteer grassroots organizations (*organizaciones de masa*). Eventually involving approximately half of the adult population, these included the Sandinista Defense Committees (CDSs), the Sandinista women's organization (AMNLAE), the Sandinista Youth (JS-19), the Association of Rural Workers (ATC), the Sandinista Workers Central (CST), and the National Union of (Small) Farmers and Cattlemen (UNAG).

The grassroots organizations, especially the neighborhood CDSs, were bitterly criticized by disgruntled Nicaraguans and detractors in the United States as being little more than vigilante committees or gangs of thugs ("*turbas*") acting as mindless puppets of their Sandinista masters. Although there were occasional excesses—such as a few instances of disruption of opposition political activities and one brief occupation of fundamentalist Protestant church buildings—no overall pattern of behavior emerged that would justify in any way such an Orwellian picture of Sandinista Nicaragua.

On the contrary, the grassroots organizations, whose behavior

108

Grassroots mobilization and mass participation. (*Above*) Liberation theologist Teófilo Cabestrero (at right) takes notes as lay Catholic Delegates of the Word discuss their experiences in teaching the "social gospel" in rural Nicaragua. (*Below*) Leaders of UNAG (The National Union of [Small] Farmers and Cattlemen) from the region around Estelí conduct an end-of-the-year meeting to assess their success and failure in meeting the goals they had set for themselves at the beginning of the year. (Photos by the author)

was in fact normally orderly and correct, actually served numerous functions of crucial importance to the new society. One of these *was* vigilance. After all, the country was under attack. It was only fitting that the people for whom this revolution was being carried out would have the opportunity to defend it against subversion. In addition to helping block the formation of an internal "fifth column," the mass organizations (especially the CDS) conducted *vigilancia revolucionaria*, a sort of neighborhood crime watch that spectacularly reduced the incidence of common violence and petty crime. Second, the grassroots organizations were also facilitators. Their role in mobilizing the enthusiastic voluntary participation of hundreds of thousands of Nicaraguans was an indispensable boost to the literacy crusade, health and housing programs, the organization of sports and cultural activities, the production and distribution of food, and the reactivation of the economy. Third, these organizations were vehicles for citizen input and participation. Through them hundreds of thousands of ordinary citizens learned how to hold meetings, elect leaders, debate issues, make collective decisions, and implement projects. Fourth, they frequently channeled feedback about common concerns to the government. For instance, demonstrations and other pressure from the ATC were clearly responsible for an important shift in government policy away from a heavy emphasis on state farms toward a policy of land distribution to peasant cooperatives and individual small-holders. Finally, these organizations played a crucial role in political socialization. All societies have ways of transmitting from generation to generation a common body of knowledge and attitudes toward national history, heroes, values, and principles. Through group activity and discussion, the new grassroots organizations helped replace old Somoza era values with ones appropriate to a more sovereign, just, and humane society.

The Sandinist armed forces were also an important pillar of the new system. Forged in long years of difficult struggle against the Somozas, they were explicitly Sandinista and therefore very unlikely to stage a coup against their own government—a phenomenon quite common elsewhere in Latin America. During the years of guerrilla warfare and throughout the eighteen-month War of Liberation, the FSLN army was vastly outnumbered and outgunned by Somoza's U.S.-trained and -equipped National Guard. Numbering only a few hundred during the urban uprisings of September 1978, the regular FSLN forces had grown to only a few thousand by the beginning of the Final Offensive of June 1979. It is remarkable that one unit of this tiny force was able to launch the attack on Managua with only "approximately 125 weapons of war [FALs, M-1s, M-16s, Uzis, Galils,

In July of 1979 members of the rebel militias pose for the author at a checkpoint near the northern town of Condega. The makeshift uniforms and old M-1 weapon were fairly typical of the urban militias.

and the like] and ten light machine guns and bazookas."[6] The FSLN won the war not because of its military superiority, but because it was convinced of the rightness of its cause and enjoyed the support of most Nicaraguans. The combination of a lean but well-trained and dedicated guerrilla army and massive urban insurgency was more than Somoza's corrupt and demoralized army could withstand.

At the time of the victory, the guerrilla army grew precipitously. In the final days of the war, many thousands of urban insurgents "joined" the FSLN army by simply "liberating" weapons and uniforms from the thousands of surrendering or fleeing guardsmen. This influx of raw, untrained soldiers was both a blessing and a problem. It allowed the new government to provide police and emergency services from the very start. Indeed, as I traveled through Nicaragua in the week following the victory, I was impressed by the organization, efficiency, and very real courtesy of the relatively untrained young people who were performing police and security functions. Yet, there were problems. Whereas most of the veteran members of the FSLN army had been trained not only in military skills but also in the role

A seventeen-year-old veteran—hero of the FSLN Army—and a friend pose for the author in November 1979. His Belgian FAL automatic rifle was the favorite weapon of the small regular guerrilla army.

of the new armed forces and the social mission of the revolution, the new volunteers had not. In the first year after the liberation, therefore, emphasis was placed on weeding out undisciplined riffraff and training the rest to be politically and socially conscious and humane guardians of the revolution. In regular training and during "criticism and self-criticism" sessions held in the evenings, the young men and women of the new armed forces were reminded that, in contrast to the hated National Guard, their role was to act as servants, friends, and protectors of the people.

In the first year, the FSLN's major military concern appears to have been to build a conventional military establishment, with standardized equipment, roughly equivalent to the military institutions of most other Central American countries. However, as noted earlier,

Posters and murals as vehicles of political and social education. (*Upper left*) A mural depicts the popular insurrection
while a billboard (*lower left*) states proudly "Today the new
dawn ceased to be an illusion" (the portraits are of Sandino
and Carlos Fonseca). Another billboard (*upper right*) stresses
the virtues of breast feeding, proclaiming "Your milk is
insubstitutible and it arrives with love." (Photos by the
author)

the election of Ronald Reagan in November 1980 triggered a new type of military buildup in Nicaragua. Designed not only to contain a constantly growing U.S.-sponsored *contra* army but also to make a U.S. invasion so costly to the invader that it would, they hoped, not take place, this buildup moved in lockstep with the escalating U.S. threat.

In the ensuing years, the Sandinist armed forces proved highly successful in containing the *contra* invasion. This was so, in part, because the Sandinista Army and the Sandinista Militias had a keen sense of what they were fighting for and whom they were fighting against. Although Ronald Reagan would label the *contras* "Freedom Fighters," their brutal behavior toward civilians made them appear to be little more than a resuscitated version of Somoza's old National Guard. The fact that, as of 1985, forty-six of the forty-eight officers of the Nicaraguan Democratic Forces (FDN—the main *contra* group) were former Somoza Guard officers did little to dispel that impression.[7]

Although the major functions of the Sandinist armed forces were national defense and internal security, they also played a role in political socialization. In undergoing military training and serving in their country's armed forces, hundreds of thousands of men and women of all ages received, at one time or another, additional exposure to the values, principles, and goals of the Sandinista revolution—perhaps one of the reasons for which the elite groups were so bitterly opposed to the military draft instituted in 1983.

Although the Sandinistas enjoyed a tremendous political advantage in post-Somoza Nicaragua, they were by no means unopposed. Indeed, they faced tenacious resistance from several quarters—a resistance wielded more by certain interest groups than by formal political parties. The non-Sandinista parties that originated or re-emerged during the first six years of the new system lacked leadership, organizational capacity, and, most important, grassroots support. On the right were the Nicaraguan Social Christian party (PSCN), the Social Democratic party (PSD), and the Constitutional Liberal party (PLC). In the center were the Democratic Conservative party (PCD), the Popular Social Christian party (PPSC), and the Independent Liberal party (PLI). To the left of these, and of the Sandinistas, were the Nicaraguan Socialist party (PSN), the Marxist-Leninist Popular Action Movement (MAP-ML), and the Nicaraguan Communist party (PCN). Closely attached to several of the opposition parties were the small labor unions once tolerated by Somoza: the AFL-CIO–oriented Confederation of Labor Unity (CUS) and the Social Christian Confederation of Workers of Nicaragua (CTN).

At first, party opposition came from the right and part of the left, whereas some of the center and left supported the government. The PPSC, the PLI, and the PSN actually joined the FSLN in a progovernment coalition, the Revolutionary Patriotic Front (FPR); and the PCD, while not part of that coalition, furnished one member of the last Junta, Rafael Córdoba Rivas. However, one of the effects of the 1984 electoral campaign was that, although the parties of the right—grouped in something called the Ramiro Sacasa Democratic Coordinating Committee (CDRS, or *la Coordinadora* for short)— abstained in an effort to delegitimize the process, the progovernment coalition disintegrated and each member party, along with the PCD, the MAP-ML, and the PCN, ran their own candidates in opposition to the FSLN. The bitter invective that came out of that campaign made it very unlikely that the old FPR coalition could ever be resurrected.

The most important opposition, however, came from the conservative hierarchy of the Catholic church and from the business community. The church in Sandinista Nicaragua—never very unified even before the revolution—became badly divided thereafter. On the one hand, a number of lower-level clergy, taking seriously the idea of a preferential option for the poor, accepted posts in the new government (including the Ministries of Culture and Foreign Affairs and the directorship of the 1980 National Literacy Crusade) or continued to work closely with poor communities. At the same time, most of the hierarchy, led by Archbishop Miguel Obando y Bravo, apparently fearing that their authority might be undermined by the mass movement within both the church and Nicaraguan society, recoiled from the revolutionary process. Although the government guaranteed freedom of religion and even tried to demonstrate its respect for Nicaraguan religiosity by promoting religious celebrations, inviting a visit by the Pope, and retaining "In God We Trust" on newly minted Sandinista coins, Obando and other bishops moved to separate the church from the revolution. They attempted unsuccessfully to force all clergy out of public office; they arranged for the removal from the country of many prerevolutionary foreign clergy and for the reassignment of similarly minded native priests; they denounced popularly oriented church organizations; and, eventually, they even managed to get many clergy to refuse to conduct burial services for members of the Sandinist armed forces killed in clashes with the *contras*. Given the intense religious identification of the Nicaraguan people, the church remained an important political factor. Its influence, however, was significantly diminished by its lack of unity.

The other important traditional power contender was the private sector. After 1979, its major political instrument was COSEP. The

FSLN's decision to preserve a mixed economy in which the bulk of production would remain in the hands of the private sector automatically meant that COSEP and the class it represented retained some political, as well as significant economic, power. This situation created important political strains in revolutionary Nicaragua. Although the government made significant concessions to the moneyed elite that included the provision of reactivation loans, an intermittent effort at dialogue, and the inclusion of COSEP in the Council of State, much of the private sector—convinced from the start that "communism" was just around the corner—was openly hostile in political matters and only grudgingly cooperative in the economic realm. Its political behavior—opposition to the literacy crusade, hostility toward the mass organizations, and insistence on the "depoliticization" of the military—reflected a desire to return Nicaragua to the prerevolutionary status quo.

THE 1984 ELECTIONS AND THE
NEW GOVERNMENTAL SYSTEM

The system of national government that existed during the first five years was a temporary one, designed simply to carry Nicaragua through a difficult period of transition until more permanent institutions could be devised. Even prior to their victory, the Sandinistas had indicated that their country's governmental institutions would ultimately be based on free elections. In the wake of the Triumph, they talked of holding elections almost immediately. At that point, opposition groups complained that to do so would be unfair given Sandinista popularity in the afterglow of the victory. At the close of the literacy crusade in August 1980, the Sandinistas announced that elections would be held in 1985. Then, and over the next three years, the opposition complained that 1985 was too distant and that the Sandinistas were, in fact, betraying their promise to hold elections. This theme was reiterated by candidate, and then president-elect, Ronald Reagan in 1980 and by spokespersons for the new U.S. administration throughout the following three years.

In the meantime, little public notice was given to the methodical and careful preparations for the promised election, then under way in Nicaragua. Commissions were sent to various parts of the world (including Western Europe and the United States) to study party laws and electoral procedures. Following consultation among all parties and groups willing to engage in dialogue, a Parties Law and an Electoral Law were drafted and enacted. In December 1983, the Directorate announced that the election would be moved to 1984, and the following month the exact date (November 4) was set. This time, the Nicaraguan opposition and official Washington decried the fact that the election—still ten months away—was being scheduled too soon. There would be little time, they argued, for the opposition to organize an effective campaign. The whole affair would be a "Soviet-style farce."

In an apparent attempt to make this description of things come true and, hence, to delegitimize the election, the Reagan administration then proceeded to interfere extensively in the Nicaraguan electoral process. Arturo Cruz, an unannounced "candidate" of the right-wing Coordinadora Democrática coalition (CDRS), was hyped as the only viable opposition candidate. The U.S. media picked up and reiterated this theme. In fact, the Cruz "candidacy" appears to have been a charade from the start. It is unlikely that the Coordinadora ever had much potential voter strength. In addition, as one unnamed "senior" Reagan administration "official" reportedly said, "The Administration never contemplated letting Cruz stay in the race, because then the Sandinistas could justifiably claim that the elections were legitimate, making it much harder to oppose the Nicaraguan government."[8] And another well-informed U.S. official speculated candidly that, as of December 1983, "they [Cruz and the Coordinadora] had already decided not to participate."[9] Nevertheless, Cruz proceeded to carry on a highly publicized cat-and-mouse game in which he went to Nicaragua, held political rallies, and set "conditions" for formal participation, but never actually registered as a candidate in spite of the fact that many of his conditions were met and the deadline for candidate registration was extended twice on his behalf.

Meanwhile U.S. officials in Nicaragua were working feverishly behind the scenes to cajole, counsel, pressure, and, reportedly, bribe the candidates of the six opposition parties that were formally registered in the election to withdraw.[10] Their efforts were not very successful. The PLI presidential candidate, Virgilio Godoy, withdrew too late to be legally removed from the ballot, and last-minute splits within the PCD over the issue of participation only marginally weakened the involvement of that party. In the end, the conclusion of impartial and authoritative election observer delegations—such as those sent by the British Parliament and House of Lords, the Irish Parliament, the Dutch Government, the Socialist International (the organization of Western European Social Democratic parties), and the U.S.-based Latin American Studies Association—was that the election had been competitive and meaningful.[11]

These international observers also agreed that the process through which the votes had been cast and counted on election day was beyond reproach. The Nicaraguan electoral law, as previously noted, drew heavily from Western European practices. The government had been given extensive direct technical assistance by members of the Swedish Electoral Commission.

In addition, the Nicaraguan elections clearly benefited from the fact that the unsavory example of the 1984 Salvadoran elections was still fresh in people's minds. In El Salvador, citizens were required by law to vote. Their citizen identification cards, which Salvadorans must carry at all times, were stamped at the voting place to indicate that they had, indeed, voted. Furthermore, the ballots used in El Salvador, like those used in Nicaragua under the Somozas, were translucent so that even when folded they did not ensure a secret vote. Moreover, some voting booths were not fully curtained and all ballot boxes were made of clear acrylic plastic. Finally, there were relatively few voting places. While this fact made for highly filmable scenes of long lines of Salvadorans supposedly registering their faith in the "democratic process," it also caused considerable unnecessary inconvenience, chaos, and numerous irregularities.

In Nicaragua, *all* of these election-day defects were avoided. Voting was not obligatory. There was no stamping of citizen ID cards (Nicaragua has no national system of identification) or any other lasting way of distinguishing between voters and nonvoters. The ballots had dark bands across the back of the section in which voters were to mark their "X." All voting places had curtains from floor to ceiling. The ballot boxes were made of wood. And there were 3,892 voting places conveniently located throughout the country. Many Nicaraguans did line up long before the polls opened, but for the most part they did not have to wait long after the voting began. The process I witnessed as part of the LASA Observer Delegation (going unescorted, unannounced, and at random to a number of polling places) was orderly and clean.

When asked by the LASA delegation if the United States were not applying a double standard in its evaluation of the 1984 elections in El Salvador and Nicaragua, a U.S. diplomat replied in a pique: "The United States is not obliged to apply the same standard of judgment to a country whose government is avowedly hostile to the U.S. as for a country, like El Salvador, where it is not. These people [the Sandinistas] could bring about a situation in Central America which could pose a threat to U.S. security. That allows us to change our yardstick."[12]

There are some superficially valid criticisms of the Nicaraguan elections, however. First, although censorship of the printed media during the campaign period was drastically reduced, it was not completely eliminated. And there were instances in which angry pro-Sandinista crowds—critics called them *turbas* ("mobs")—disrupted opposition political rallies. However, it should be noted that what *was* published in *La Prensa* was bitterly and consistently critical of the Sandinistas and that a half hour on television and 45 minutes on Sandinista radio were set aside free of charge at prime time every evening during the electoral period for uncensored comment and campaign speeches by opposition parties and candidates. Additional time was also available for purchase. Moreover, the internationally hyped disruptions of opposition meetings by Sandinista *turbas* actually occurred in only "five instances out of some 250 rallies during the campaign period; that is, [they] did not constitute a pattern of activity but [were], rather, the exception."[13]

In the end, as noted earlier, 75 percent of the Nicaraguan electorate chose to vote even though no one was obliged or intimidated to do so; only 6 percent of those who voted spoiled their ballots, although that would have been an excellent way of anonymously registering opposition; and 63 percent of all voters (67 percent of those casting valid ballots) voted Sandinista, even though there were three opposition parties each to the right and the left of the FSLN. By any objective measure, then, the Sandinistas had won a clean, honest, *landslide* victory.

The elections gave Nicaragua a president (Daniel Ortega), a vice-president (Sergio Ramírez), and a 96-person National (Constituent) Assembly. Inaugurated in January 1985, all elected officials were to hold office for six years unless the Assembly decided otherwise.

The National Assembly had a variety of functions, but clearly the most important was that of producing a constitution. U.S. citizens familiar with their president's description of Nicaragua as a "totalitarian dungeon" might imagine that the FSLN would simply write a constitution and present it to the Assembly to be rubber-stamped. But there was almost no possibility that this was going to take place. The people who had designed the electoral law had deliberately selected a Western European system of proportional representation that tended to overrepresent minority parties. In addition, they had included a provision whereby all losing presidential candidates would get seats in the Assembly. The end result was that while the Sandinistas got 61 seats, the opposition parties got a substantial 35 (PCD, 14; PLI, 9; PPSC, 6; PSN, 2; PCN, 2; MAP-ML, 2). This meant that the FSLN had just barely the 60 percent necessary to pass the constitution. Furthermore, the same practical considerations that had caused the Sandinistas to pursue dialogue, feedback, and pluralism during the

Government of National Reconstruction were very much present as the constitution was being written.

During the first six months of its existence, the Assembly began the process of producing a constitution. A plan of action was adopted. As in the case of the Parties and Electoral Laws, delegations were to be sent to various parts of the world (again, including the United States and Western Europe) to study constitutions and consult with foreign constitutional experts. A draft of the constitution was to be prepared by late 1985. In 1986, copies of this document would be distributed throughout the country, and a process of "National Consultation" would begin. Public meetings would be held, and feedback from them and the various interest groups would be taken into consideration as the final version was drawn up. The revised draft would then face an up-down vote of the Assembly as a whole.[14] Finally, although such an additional step is not normally considered necessary in the case of a constitution passed by an elected constituent assembly, there was a possibility according to informed sources that this fundamental law might also be submitted for approval to the Nicaraguan people in a referendum.

In six years, Nicaragua had come a long way in institutionalizing a governmental system based on the participation and consent of the governed. However, it remained to be seen whether this unique experiment in genuine self-government would be allowed to survive.

NOTES

1. For an examination of the history and activities of this party as of the late 1960s, see Thomas W. Walker, *The Christian Democratic Movement in Nicaragua* (Tucson: University of Arizona Press, 1970).

2. Small wonder that few people in Nicaragua were particularly saddened to hear fourteen months later that Somoza's life of comfortable exile in Paraguay had ended in a crescendo of bazooka and automatic weapon fire. (Though the government of Paraguayan dictator Alfredo Stroessner subsequently captured or killed several Argentine "terrorists" who it claimed were responsible for the killing, circumstantial evidence points to the involvement of high-ranking officers in Stroessner's own military who may have been upset at Somoza's alleged effort to elbow his way into the lucrative drug smuggling business previously dominated by those officers.)

3. "Afirma el Comandante Bayardo Arce, 'El Consejo de Estado garantiza el Pluralismo Político,'" *Patria Libre*, vol. 4 (May 1980), p. 22.

4. John A. Booth, "The National Governmental System," in Thomas W. Walker, ed., *Nicaragua: The First Five Years* (New York: Praeger Publishers, 1985), p. 39. For more detailed discussion of a number of other topics covered in this section, see (1) Charles Downs, "Local and Regional Government,"

(2) Luis Héctor Serra, "The Grass-Roots Organizations," (3) Stephen M. Gorman and Thomas W. Walker, "The Armed Forces," (4) Michael Dodson and Laura O'Shaughnessy, "Religion and Politics," and (5) Dennis Gilbert, "The Bourgeoisie," in Walker, ed., *Nicaragua: The First Five Years*, pp. 45–144, 163–182.

5. For a critical examination of the TPAs see Lawyers Committee for International Human Rights, *Nicaragua: Revolutionary Justice—A Report on Human Rights and the Judicial System* (New York and Washington, D.C.: LCIHR, 1985), pp. 33–93.

6. Comandante Carlos Nuñez Téllez, *Un Pueblo en Armas* (Managua: Secretaría Nacional de Propaganda y Educación Política del FSLN, 1980), p. 26.

7. Arms Control and Foreign Policy Caucus, U.S. House of Representatives, "Who Are the Contras?" *Congressional Record*, 131, 48 (Daily Edition, April 23, 1985), H2335.

8. "U.S. Role in Nicaraguan Vote Disputed," *New York Times* (October 21, 1984).

9. The Latin American Studies Association, *The Electoral Process in Nicaragua: Domestic and International Influences* (Austin: LASA, 1984), p. 30.

10. Ibid., pp. 30, 31.

11. For the bibliographical information on the European reports see note 24 in Chapter 3.

12. LASA, *The Electoral Process*, p. 32.

13. Americas Watch, *Human Rights in Nicaragua: Reagan, Rhetoric and Reality* (New York: Americas Watch, 1985), p. 62.

14. Interview with Milú Vargas, General Director of Advisors to the National Assembly, National Assembly, Managua, June 25, 1985.

7

The International Dimension

In November 1979, as I deplaned at Managua's Augusto César Sandino International Airport on my second visit to Nicaragua since the liberation, I stopped to gaze at a large new sign on the main terminal building: "Welcome to Free Nicaragua." For some international visitors, this greeting may have held little significance. For others, it probably reinforced deep-seated fears and suspicions. But for one who had studied and empathized with the plight of the Nicaraguan people for over a decade, this proud salutation was rich with bittersweet meaning. After four-and-a-half centuries of foreign domination and abuse, the Nicaraguan people had finally won the right to proclaim themselves sovereign and independent—a stirring and historic accomplishment. Yet one could not help wondering if it could last. Could a tiny republic of then barely 2.5 million people located deep within the geopolitical sphere of influence of one of the world's superpowers actually set an independent course for itself? Six years later, the answer to this question was still by no means clear.

NICARAGUA AS A CLIENT STATE

As the reader will probably have gathered from the historical chapters of this book, real sovereignty was almost a totally new experience for Nicaragua. During its first half century of "independence," Nicaragua had been buffetted by the conflicting commercial and geopolitical interests of the United States and Great Britain. In the latter part of the nineteenth century, the modernizing liberal dictator, José Santos Zelaya, had briefly championed the cause of Nicaraguan and Central American self-determination. The British had been dislodged from the Atlantic territories; the cause of Central American unity had been revived; U.S. overtures for a very concessionary Nicaraguan canal treaty had been rejected; and an effort had been made to diversify the country's international trade relationship in order to reduce dependence on the United States. However, as we saw, the United States eventually reacted to Zelaya's independent attitude—and especially to the possibility that he might let other international interests build a canal that would compete with the newly constructed U.S. waterway at Panama—by conspiring with Zelaya's Conservative opposition and backing them militarily in their effort to overthrow Zelaya and then to stay in power as a minority party.

During the first third of the twentieth century, Nicaragua's tiny privileged elite—Conservative and Liberal alike—came to realize that its narrow class interests could best be pursued through a subservient, symbiotic relationship with the United States. The Conservatives were the first to get the message. They would never have succeeded in their rebellion against the central government in 1909, nor defeated Benjamín Zeledón's nationalist forces in 1912, had it not been for direct U.S. military intervention. Accordingly, they learned to address their foreign protectors in a groveling and obsequious manner. For instance, after the defeat of Zeledón, a group of Conservatives of "the highest social, political, and financial standing" sent the local commander of the marines a message of thanks that was clearly tailored to appeal to the ethnocentric and chauvinistic interpretation of Central American reality prevalent in the United States at that time.

> The lamentable situation of these countries, perturbed by constant uprisings, is all the sadder when we consider their proximity to the great American nation, which, founded on wise institutions and inspired by the spirit of liberty and justice, marches at the head of the destiny of humanity. Thus the presence of the American troops among us marks an era of peace for this Republic because she now has spread over us the protecting influence of her altruistic policy.[1]

The Conservative elite also ingratiated itself to the Americans by taking loans with private U.S. banks, allowing the occupiers to run many aspects of the country's public finances, and giving their protectors almost exactly the type of concessionary canal treaty Zelaya had vehemently rejected as injurious to the national interest. Among other things, the Bryan-Chamorro Treaty of 1916 allowed the United States to corner the rights to a Nicaraguan canal, thus insuring that the new U.S. waterway through Panama could continue to operate without competition.

By the late 1920s, the Liberal elite also came to realize that its class interests could best be promoted by cultivating a symbiotic relationship with the United States. After the United States blocked one last attempt to remove the Conservatives by force, all of the major Liberal leaders, except Augusto César Sandino, bowed to the inevitable and endorsed the U.S.-sponsored Peace of Tipitapa in May 1927. Having done so, they won the U.S.-sponsored presidential elections of 1928 and 1932.

The behavior of the Liberal and Conservative client governments that nominally ruled Nicaragua during the second U.S. occupation (from 1926 to 1933) was obsequiously pro-American. The occupiers continued to play a key role in the financial affairs of the country. The U.S.-trained, -equipped, and -officered "Nicaraguan" National Guard was rapidly developed and expanded as an immediate response to Sandinist "banditry" and as a long-range answer to the problem of insuring pro-U.S. stability in the region.

One of the clearest examples of the subservient character of these governments can be seen in Nicaragua's docile ratification of the very unfavorable Barcenas Meneses–Esguerra Treaty of 1928. As a result of this treaty, Nicaragua relinquished to Colombia the Providencia and San Andrés islands and certain keys off Nicaragua's Atlantic coast. Though even a cursory glance at a map of the Caribbean would tend to verify Nicaragua's historic right to these territories, Colombia had long maintained a conflicting claim based on rather vague policing authority granted its colonial predecessor by the Spanish crown. While it was certainly not in Nicaragua's interest to relinquish these possessions, the United States benefited in two ways. First, the treaty helped assuage long-simmering Colombian resentment over U.S. connivance and military involvement in the independence of the former Colombian province of Panama in 1903. Then, too, it voided additional Colombian claims that had tended to cloud the validity of certain U.S. rights under the Bryan-Chamorro Treaty.

The Role of the Somozas

While it is clear that Nicaragua's status as a client state had developed long before the Somozas took power, it is also true that Anastasio Somoza García and his two sons did much to refine that undignified relationship. Throughout most of the Somoza period, Nicaraguan and U.S. foreign policy were virtually indistinguishable. As a bitter Anastasio Somoza Debayle remarked shortly after his overthrow: "I stood back to back with the U.S. and gave my ally all the support I could muster. . . . [no] president anywhere supported the policies of the United States more devoutly than I did. . . . no such loyalty existed anywhere."[2]

The relationship was one of mutual benefit. The Somozas tailored their foreign policy to the interests of their international protector and the United States, in turn, lavished various favors on its client. Throughout the whole affair, the interested parties whose aspirations and needs were consistently ignored were the citizens of Nicaragua. U.S. personnel occasionally may have experienced some queasiness over the nature of the system they were supporting, but as Franklin Delano Roosevelt is said to have remarked at one point, "Somoza might be an S.O.B., but he is *our* S.O.B."

For their part, the Somozas served the perceived foreign policy interests of the United States in a number of ways. In the United Nations and other international forums, they consistently voted with the United States. They leased military bases to the United States during the Second World War. They allowed Nicaraguan territory to be used as a training and staging area for CIA-sponsored invasions of Guatemala (1954) and Cuba (Bay of Pigs, 1961). They sent Nicaraguan national guardsmen to aid in the U.S. occupation of the Dominican Republic in 1965. And they even offered to send troops to Korea and Vietnam.

In the late 1960s and early 1970s, the last of the Somozas, Anastasio Somoza Debayle, also served U.S. interests as a surrogate enforcer of stability in Central America. In 1964, early in the Alliance for Progress, the Pentagon persuaded the military dictators of Central America to form the Central American Defense Council (CONDECA) to coordinate the enforcement of stability in order, theoretically, that social and economic development could take place. By the late 1960s and early 1970s, the warped nature of dependent economic "development" and the near total absence of beneficial social change led to increased social unrest that, in turn, apparently caused the United States to decide to rely more heavily on brute military control.[3] In these circumstances, Somoza, the dean of Central America's dictators and a rabid anti-Communist, naturally became the principal figure in CONDECA. Under his leadership, joint maneuvers were held, guerrilla foci were located and wiped out, and, for awhile, the status quo was preserved.

Nicaragua, under the Somozas, also served U.S. economic interests. While it is true that U.S. investments in that country were never very significant from the U.S. point of view, it is also a fact that the generally laissez faire economic philosophy of the Somozas strayed little, if at all, from that espoused by the developmentalist economists in the State Department. In more concrete terms, Anastasio

Somoza Debayle, in the early 1970s, protected U.S. economic interests at his own country's expense by helping to sabotage Latin American schemes to create coffee and banana cartels for the enforcement of higher commodity prices.

In spite of all this, however, the Somozas were never quite willing to take U.S. "friendship" for granted. They also engaged in an extensive and well-financed propaganda and lobbying campaign in the United States. Millions of dollars were paid to U.S. public relations firms to create a favorable image of their regime among Americans and full-time professional lobbyists devoted considerable effort to the manipulation of U.S. politicians at all levels.[4] As a result, the Somozas could always count on the fervent support of a large number of U.S. congressmen and senators. Some of these individuals undoubtedly behaved as they did out of honest conviction. However, the subsequent indictment and/or conviction of some prominent members of the so-called Somoza Lobby on charges related to Abscam and other corrupt activities lends credence to long-standing suspicions that more personal and material motivations may have been operative in some cases.

In return for their loyalty, the Somozas received extensive support from the United States. After the beginning of the Alliance for Progress, hundreds of millions of dollars in U.S. loans and grants-in-aid were lavished on Nicaragua, ostensibly to help in various high-sounding social and economic development projects. After the 1972 earthquake, there were additional large infusions of funds destined, supposedly, for relief and reconstruction. In fact, of course, most of the money simply evaporated. Social projects carried out by the Somozas were trivial, most of Managua remained an unreconstructed moonscape, and the positive impact of such economic "development" as did take place fell mainly on the Somozas and a small privileged elite. Yet, since the real purpose of the aid was political rather than social, Washington continued to pour taxpayers' dollars down the Somoza rathole until the day the dictator was finally ousted.

The remarkable inconsistencies in logic underlying the U.S. aid program for Nicaragua were clearly demonstrated in the spring of 1978 when the beleaguered Somoza dictatorship was sent yet another infusion of funds "to meet basic human needs." By that time, the U.S. aid program was so unpopular among most Nicaraguans that a lengthy in-house debate actually took place in the State Department over the questions of whether or not to attempt to send the aid without a public announcement. Finally, it was decided to give the ambassador the go-ahead to announce the aid, as it was felt that, even if secrecy were attempted, someone in Nicaragua would surely leak the information, making the U.S. position even more untenable.[5]

The United States also gave the Nicaraguan National Guard massive assistance, including training, in-country advising, arms, ammunition, and equipment. Indeed, the National Guard was the most heavily U.S.-trained military establishment in Latin America. More members of Somoza's guard had received military training in the United States or at U.S. bases in the Canal Zone than any other military establishment in Latin America,[6] including that of Brazil, a country approximately fifty times larger in population. Virtually all guard officers were U.S.-trained. In reality, then, there was very little that was either "Nicaraguan" or "national" about the Nicaraguan National Guard.

Finally, the United States gave the Somozas considerable political support. With a few exceptions, U.S. ambassadors to Nicaragua were usually individuals of very low professional qualifications who were easily co-opted and manipulated by the family. They tended to act more as agents and cronies of the Somozas than as envoys of the people of the United States to the people of Nicaragua. The two most clear-cut examples are those of Thomas Whelan (1951–1961) and Turner Shelton (1970–1975).

The owner of a grain and potato warehouse and one-time chairman of the Republican party of North Dakota, Whelan received his ambassadorship during the Truman administration shortly after William Langer, chairman of the Senate Judiciary Committee, threatened to block all administration legislation until such time as someone from North Dakota, Langer's home state, received an ambassadorship, a post never before held by a North Dakotan.[7] Although he never learned to speak Spanish, Whelan quickly became an intimate of the Somoza family. When Somoza García was gunned down in 1956, Whelan saw to it that the grave condition of the dictator as he lay dying in a hospital in Panama was not immediately made public. In doing so, he gave Luis and Anastasio time to consolidate their control over Nicaragua. Thereafter, he became a second father to the young Somozas. Years later, a former top adviser to Luis commented nostalgically to me that "He was *our* ambassador."[8]

The case of Turner Shelton is certainly no more uplifting than that of Whelan. An undistinguished, about-to-be-retired foreign service officer, Shelton apparently owed his appointment as ambassador to his friendship with, and campaign contributions to, Richard Nixon. Former consul general to Nassau, he had close ties with Bebe Rebozo and Howard Hughes. Indeed, he later arranged for Hughes to set up residence in Managua. Like Whelan, Shelton spoke no Spanish, but quickly became an intimate friend of the Somozas. It was he who helped arrange the Somoza-Agüero pact of 1971, which enabled Somoza to retain control of the country beyond his original term of office. At the time of the earthquake, when it became apparent that Somoza's personal guard had been thrown into such temporary disarray that it could no longer protect the dictator, Shelton immediately arranged for 600 armed U.S. troops to be flown from the Canal Zone and stationed on the grounds of Somoza's residence to "help in the relief effort." Shelton's incredible callousness to the suffering of the quake victims and his initial reluctance to offer his palatial ambassadorial residence as a temporary site to house embassy operations were so scandalous that Secretary of State Henry Kissinger eventually saw fit to rebuke him. Even so, his ultimate removal from Managua was delayed until 1975, apparently the result of active lobbying by his friend, Anastasio Somoza.

Somoza and Carter

After the overthrow of Somoza, there was a tendency in the United States either to credit or to blame the administration of Jimmy Carter for consciously promoting the downfall of the Somoza system. Such an assertion is unwarranted. It is highly doubtful that the Carter administration ever desired the overthrow of the Somoza system, much less the coming to power of the FSLN. Though the administration's behavior may have contributed to that outcome, the effect was purely unintended.

When it came to office in 1977, the Carter administration was intent on demonstrating that its much-publicized human rights policy could, indeed, find practical application. Unfortunately, the promotion of human rights by the United States was deemed impractical in many parts of the world for strategic and political reasons. However, this was not the case in Nicaragua. There, it was felt that the United States could push human rights without jeopardizing its strategic or economic interests. Unlike some other Latin American dictators, Somoza was sure to follow orders. Since the administration had been assured that the FSLN guerrilla threat had been crushed by Somoza's counteroffensive of the previous two-and-a-half years, it felt that a rights crusade could be implemented without endangering the stability of the system as a whole.

As it turned out, this perception of Nicaraguan reality was badly flawed. Washington was correct in expecting that Somoza would follow orders. In 1977, the administration was successful in getting him to call off the National Guard's campaign of terror against the peasantry and to lift the state of siege and reinstate limited freedom of the press. On the other hand, Washington made two fundamental errors in judgment. First, it underestimated the popularity and re-silience of the Sandinist Front of National Liberation. Second, it failed to perceive the fact that an artificial injection of civil and political liberties into a system built on the denial of basic social and economic justice can have a highly destabilizing effect.

The Carter team learned its lesson the hard way. By the end of 1977, it was clear not only that the FSLN had not been wiped out but that it was actually receiving increasingly wide support from important and very vocal civilian groups. Alarmed by this totally unexpected situation, the administration began downplaying its human rights campaign and maneuvering for a peaceful solution that would preserve the National Guard and the old elite while at the same time blocking the FSLN. Accordingly, the human rights report on Nicaragua that the State Department sent to Congress early in 1978 was essentially a whitewash; the administration wanted congressional approval for its economic and military aid packages for that country. In addition, even as the War of Liberation was beginning, U.S. diplomatic personnel were urging Nicaraguans to eschew violence and wait for the next Somoza-run elections in 1981. That summer, at the urging of the National Security Council, Carter even went so far as to send Somoza the infamous congratulatory letter regarding the dictator's promises to improve his performance in the area of human rights. Then came the National Palace operation of August 1978 and the massive urban uprising the following month. Extremely worried, the administration promoted an Organization of American States (OAS) effort at mediation in which an attempt was made to get Somoza and representatives of the privileged elite to agree to a solution that would have removed Somoza, preserved the guard and Somoza's Liberal party, and excluded the broad-based coalition led by the FSLN. Finally, in the summer of 1979, as the FSLN closed in on Managua in its Final Offensive, the United States dropped all pretenses and officially requested the OAS to send a peacekeeping force (à la Dominican Republic, 1965) to Nicaragua. That request, as noted earlier, was unanimously rejected.

In sum, the role of the United States in the downfall of the Somoza system was entirely unwitting. Throughout the process, the most revolutionary outcome ever envisioned by Washington was the creation of what Nicaraguans derisively refer to as "*Somocismo* without Somoza," a political system in which a slightly broader spectrum of traditional privileged elites would have participated in a superficially democratic system under the watchful eye of a cosmetically reorganized National Guard. Not until just before Somoza fell, when it had exhausted all other alternatives, did the Carter administration face reality and begin serious communication with the popularly based Sandinist Front of National Liberation.[9]

REVOLUTIONARY NICARAGUA

In an article written before the Final Offensive and subsequently published in the United States at the time of the FSLN victory, Sergio Ramírez, who was to become a central figure in the new governing junta and, later, vice-president, made some important statements.

> To think that a new, democratic government in Nicaragua might be hostile to the United States is a perverse fantasy. To think that a new and truly representative Nicaraguan government is going to insist on dignified relations with the more powerful countries. . . . is to think correctly. . . . We aspire to dignity, integrity, and international respect. . . . The United States should learn not to fear the ghosts of its past mistakes.[10]

Immediately after the liberation, both the junta and the directorate of the FSLN made various efforts to convey to U.S. authorities their "wish to develop the best possible relations and to heal the wounds inflicted as a result of Washington's historical complicity with Somoza."[11] These wounds, of course, were raw and painful. The struggle to overthrow a U.S.-backed dictator and to dismantle his U.S.-trained and -equipped army had cost Nicaragua the lives of approximately 50,000 people, or roughly 2 percent of its population. In the United States, that would be equivalent to a loss of 4.5 million people, well over 75 times the U.S. death toll in the entire Vietnam conflict. Nevertheless, given Nicaragua's geopolitical position, its economic dependence on the United States, and the remarkably widespread goodwill of Nicaraguans toward the people of the United States, it was deemed highly important to try to construct good relations with that country. Even in the exuberance of the initial victory, U.S. citizens in Nicaragua were treated courteously. There was no attack on the U.S. Embassy, nor were hostages taken. Normal relations were immediately reinstated and government and FSLN leaders traveled to the United States on goodwill missions. Nicaraguan officials turned out en masse at social affairs held by the U.S. ambassador in Managua. In all, it was hoped "that Nicaraguan-U.S. relations could develop into a model of mutual respect between a revolutionary nation and the dominant power of the western hemisphere."[12]

Though intent on developing good relations with the United States, the new government was equally determined that Nicaragua should never again become subservient to any foreign power. The concepts of self-determination and nonalignment, therefore, became the central principles of Nicaraguan foreign policy. In fewer than two months after the revolutionary victory, Nicaragua joined the Movement of Non-Aligned Countries. In doing so, it was expressing solidarity with—and seeking the support of—the peoples and governments of the Third World. It was also implementing ideas that dated back in Nicaraguan history at least to the days of Augusto César Sandino.[13]

Nonalignment, however is not construed by the members of the movement as a position of meek neutrality. While Nicaragua would never again allow itself to be a client state of any great power or permit its soil to be used for foreign military bases, East or West, it would henceforth take stands on many important issues—especially those of interest to the Third World. Yet, although Nicaragua often voted in the United Nations against the United States and with other revolutionary countries, there were important East-West issues in which its mission either abstained (e.g., Afghanistan and the Soviet downing of a Korean airliner) or sided with the United States against the USSR (e.g., the proposal to send a UN peacekeeping force to Lebanon early in 1984). And in the silly but nonetheless symbolic squabbles over the Olympics, Nicaragua decided to send teams to both the 1980 Olympics in Moscow (which the United States and many Western allies boycotted) and its 1984 sequel in Los Angeles (from which the USSR, Cuba, and most of the Socialist Bloc countries were absent). For its part, the FSLN, as a party, pursued friendly relations not only with the Communist parties of the Socialist Bloc but also with the Social Democrats of West Europe (through the Socialist International), the Liberal International, and the Permanent Conference of Political Parties of Latin America (COPPPAL). As a result of these efforts, Nicaragua avoided the international isolation that had befallen Cuba twenty years earlier. Indeed, in 1982 it was chosen by a large vote to occupy the nonpermanent UN Security Council seat traditionally assigned to Latin America.

The Sandinist policy of pursuing diplomatic relations with as many countries as possible regardless of ideology was put into motion immediately following the Triumph. Within a year, the new government had relations with a majority of the countries of the world—over twice as many as under the Somozas. In earlier times there had been no need for much diplomatic infrastructure since Nicaraguan foreign policy, for all practical purposes, had been "made in the USA." After July 1979, however, things changed so rapidly that by August of the following year an official in the Foreign Ministry informed me, with obvious pride, that the Ministry had been obliged to be moved to a large complex of buildings in order to house the various "area desks" into which it was now organized, much in the style of any modern foreign ministry.[14]

Of course, there were some problems with this global approach to foreign policy. The U.S. media and the Reagan administration consistently pointed with alarm to Nicaragua's ties with the Socialist Bloc and such radical regimes as those of Libya and Iran. At the same time, however, they generally ignored Nicaraguan success in building good working relations with many other types of countries, including the governments of Western Europe and even some of Latin America's most conservative military dictatorships. To try to counteract this distortion, the Nicaraguans were careful to make sure that most, if not all, high-level trips to Europe included stops in both Eastern Bloc *and* Western European countries. But this effort was often to no avail, as evidenced by the case of Daniel Ortega's carefully balanced trip to Europe in May 1985, which the Reagan administration, the media, and a surprisingly large number of liberals in the U.S. Congress characterized simply as "Ortega's trip to Moscow."

Then, too, the development of relations with the two Chinas initially proved problematic. The People's Republic of China at first insisted that formal ties with the mainland should be contingent on the severance of Nicaragua's long-standing relations with Taiwan. Eventually, however, although Nicaragua refused to comply, it was able to develop excellent trade relations with the PRC, which ultimately became a major purchaser of Nicaraguan cotton. Overall, Nicaragua's open approach to foreign relations seemed to produce more benefits than costs.

One of the pillars of Nicaragua's new foreign policy was the continuance and enrichment of relations with Western Europe.[15] The organization of Western Europe Social Democratic parties, the Socialist International, or SI (which in the late 1970s included the ruling parties of West Germany, Sweden, Austria, Denmark, etc.) had been very supportive of the FSLN during the War of Liberation. After the Triumph, as it became increasingly worried about possible future U.S. behavior toward Nicaragua, the SI went so far as to form an International Committee for the Defense of the Nicaraguan Revolution, which included an impressive list of SI leaders (among them former West German Chancellor Willy Brandt). The Government of National Reconstruction built on this support by frequently sending high-level delegations to Europe to explain Nicaraguan positions and to solicit aid and trade.

Nicaraguan relations with Western Europe fluctuated from country to country and from time to time. The United States, especially under Reagan, vigorously pressured its allies to diminish their ties to Nicaragua. And there were changes in European governments that affected relations with the Sandinistas. The coming to power of the Christian Democrats in Germany in 1982 was a clear loss. On the other hand, that setback was balanced by Social Democratic victories in France (1981) and Spain (1982).

Overall, however, the relationship with Western Europe remained constructive throughout the first six years. Although the United States blocked the transfer of all but a trickle of badly needed arms from Western Europe to Nicaragua, it was forced to listen to European calls for a peaceful settlement and was relatively ineffective in slowing the flow of trade and aid. Indeed, as noted earlier, when the Reagan administration hit Nicaragua with a full trade embargo in May 1985, the Western European countries expressed their disapproval not only by refusing to join but also by immediately offering Nicaragua a total of $198 million (U.S.) in new assistance. And, of course, several Western European countries had earlier played a crucial role not only in verifying the legitimacy of the 1984 electoral process but, perhaps more important, in helping to set it up in the first place.

A more universal approach to diplomacy also implied the pursuit of relations with various Communist countries both within and outside the Socialist Bloc. Logically, Nicaragua's strongest relationship was that with Cuba: The two countries had strikingly similar historical experiences in having undergone, first, foreign domination and dictatorship, then a successful guerrilla war, and finally a genuine social revolution in which sweeping programs of social change and national defense had to occur simultaneously. Almost immediately after the Triumph, Nicaragua received a number of Cuban advisers in the areas of health, education, and military training. Moreover, leaders of the two countries exchanged visits. Both before and immediately after the victory, Fidel Castro advised the Nicaraguans to preserve a private sector and retain good relations with the United States. Relations with the rest of the Socialist Bloc also advanced, but at a slower pace. Gradually, diplomatic relations were established or reopened, and agreements for trade and aid were signed.

Although the new Nicaraguan armed forces were pathetically equipped throughout 1979 and 1980, the Sandinistas saw fit to import only relatively small amounts of Socialist Bloc weaponry until well after Ronald Reagan was inaugurated in January 1981. Much effort, at first, was spent in attempting to obtain standardized equipment from less controversial sources—the United States and Western Europe. Eventually, however, when the United States not only refused to sell arms but also blocked the transfer of any significant amount of material from sources in Western Europe (an arms agreement with France signed late in 1981 was subsequently killed under intense pressure from Washington),[16] Nicaragua moved ahead with the large-scale procurement of Socialist Bloc weaponry. There was simply no alternative. Even so, the importation of such material grew as a clear response to the escalating threat from Washington.[17] And each purchase appears to have been carefully thought out with respect to its political implications. For instance, the first standardized equipment received by the Sandinista Militia were obsolete Czech BZ-52 ten-shot rifles—hardly an offensive weapon. The militia was first issued modern AK-47 automatic rifles in 1983, almost two years into the Reagan administration's CIA-directed *contra* invasion. The several dozen Soviet-built tanks that Nicaragua imported shortly after Reagan came to power were old T-54s and T-55s. These were not obtained from the manufacturer but, rather, were sent second hand from Algeria—an apparent effort to remove any political connotation. Eventually, of course, the rhythm of Socialist Bloc arms procurement picked up as the *contra* war accelerated, and repeated leaks from official sources in Washington indicated that a full-scale U.S. invasion might be in the offing.

Even as of mid-1985, Nicaragua's relationship with the Socialist Bloc was measured and practical. Trade with the Socialist Bloc stood at about 20 percent of Nicaragua's total. The Soviet Union and other countries were giving some aid, but the USSR, for one, refused to offer the hard-currency support that Nicaragua so badly needed. It had also indicated that it would not intervene militarily in Nicaragua's defense in the event of a U.S. invasion. The USSR *was*, by default, Nicaragua's major arms supplier. But at no time had it given the Sandinist armed forces an offensive capability. Nicaragua had almost no air force, little logistical infrastructure, and insufficient fuel-storage capacity to launch a serious invasion against any of its neighbors. And, even though the Reagan administration repeatedly stressed the military danger that the Sandinist armed forces purportedly posed to neighboring countries, it did so knowing that what it was saying was simply not the truth. Indeed, the Reagan administration was embarrassed in September 1982 when a subcommittee of the House Committee on Intelligence issued a staff report criticizing U.S. intelligence performance in Central America and noting in particular that, while U.S. intelligence services were publicly trumpeting Nicaragua's supposed offensive capabilities and intentions, there had been "classified briefings whose analytical judgments about Nicaragua's intentions were quite distinct from those that appeared implicit in the briefings on the buildup."[18] And the in-house assessment did not change over time. A classified intelligence report prepared in 1984 still contended that "the overall buildup [in Nicaragua] is primarily defense-oriented, and much of the recent effort has been devoted to improving counterinsurgency capabilities."[19] What is more, at no point had the Soviet Union attempted to put its own bases in Nicaragua—as Washington often warned it would. In fact, the Sandinistas had repeatedly stated categorically that they would not allow such a thing.

Nicaragua's major foreign policy problem, from the start, had been the United States.[20] As previously noted, the Carter administration had done almost all it could—short of sending troops—to block the Sandinista victory. True, after the Triumph it then tried to make the best of what it perceived to be an unwelcome situation by maintaining relations with Nicaragua, sending emergency relief, continuing non-military aid already "in the pipeline" to Somoza, and proposing an additional $75 million in new aid. However, 1980—an election year—was hardly a convenient time for a weak incumbent president to be designing a rational policy of coexistence with a new revolutionary government "in our own back yard." Hardliners in Congress had a field day with the Nicaraguan aid bill, amending it and holding it up until the second half of 1980. And although a joint report of the State Department and the Pentagon recommended a favorable reply to the Nicaraguan request to help arm its small military establishment,[21] the Carter administration rejected the idea. Such a proposal, however realistic, would have stood a scant chance in Congress. Nor were the Sandinistas particularly pleased early in 1980 when the Carter administration chose instead to build up the Honduran military while doing nothing to pressure the government of that country to disband groups of *contras* that already were allegedly being harbored in training camps in Honduras.

Some things about the Sandinistas were upsetting to Washington. Many of Nicaragua's new leaders were indeed Marxists. They had never made any attempt to hide that fact. They *were* developing relations with Cuba and other Communist countries both within and outside the Socialist Bloc. And the Sandinistas *were* using rhetoric heavily laced with buzz words—"imperialism," "capitalist exploitation," "bourgeoisie," "proletariat," "liberation," "vanguard"—which, though appropriate in their own setting, tended to unnerve U.S. decision makers having little contact with, or understanding of, Central American reality. These same individuals were further alarmed to be told over and over that the new Nicaraguan "national anthem" included a section calling upon Nicaraguans to "fight against the Yankee, the enemy of humanity." In fact, these words were a part not of the national anthem but, rather, of the FSLN battle hymn, which, like all such hymns, is a historical artifact; hence, over time, it could lose its jingoistic import just as the Marine Corps hymn, with its unfriendly reference to Mexico and Tripoli, is now a historical curiosity rather than a cause for offense to Mexicans and Arabs.

But in fairness to the Sandinistas, we must note that the new government had made considerable efforts to remain "respectable" in the eyes of Washington. These efforts were not just superficial gestures. The Sandinistas' prolonged attempt to buy badly needed arms from Western rather than Communist sources was a clear effort to avoid being unduly dependent on the Socialist Bloc. The decisions to pay Somoza's foreign debt, to preserve a mixed economy, to respect religious liberty, to allow almost complete freedom of the press until 1982, to accept U.S. aid in spite of grossly insulting conditions,[22] to create a pluralistic system of temporary government, and to forge ahead to carry out promised elections—all of these and a number of other policies were designed, at least in part, to signal the West that this was a uniquely Nicaraguan revolution worthy of being given a chance.

Be that as it may, the administration inaugurated in Washington in January 1981 showed scant interest in coexisting with the Sandinistas. There were some initial attempts at negotiation, but these were conducted in a haughty and condescending manner and against a backdrop of bellicose statements from Washington that almost seemed designed to defeat their purpose. By late 1981, the CIA-*contra* effort had been given the president's formal approval and, from then on, there was apparently no turning back. U.S. military maneuvers and infrastructural buildup in the area escalated inexorably. By 1984, upwards of 15,000 *contras* were harassing the Nicaraguan government. A year later, U.S. officials coordinating *contra* operations out of the White House were claiming a surrogate force of 20,000, which they expected to build to "35,000 in the next six months."[23]

Throughout the period of Reagan's first term, both sides claimed to be interested in a negotiated settlement. But the sincerity of these claims appears to have been rather one-sided. In the diplomatic exchanges that occurred in the second half of 1981, Nicaragua had proposed the creation of a joint Honduran-Nicaraguan border patrol to prevent illegal movement in either direction across the border. Such an arrangement would have helped address U.S. worries over alleged Nicaraguan arms shipments across Honduran territory to the guerrillas in El Salvador. The United States not only turned the proposal down but also pressured Honduras, which had initially shown interest in it, to do the same. In early 1982, after the president's December 1981 authorization of CIA-*contra* activities against Nicaragua

Nicaragua under siege. (*Upper left*) As the *contra* war grew and the threat of a U.S. invasion become ever more real, Nicaraguans of all ages and both sexes joined the militia and demanded to be armed. (*Lower left*) Members of self-defense agricultural communities in the north worked with their weapons (in this case, an AK-47) strapped to their shoulders. (*Upper right*) Urban dwellers dug L-shaped slit trenches in vacant lots and back patios. (*Lower right*) Meanwhile, from late 1983 onward, a large segment of the U.S. community in Managua held regular Thursday morning peace vigils in front of the U.S. embassy asking their government not to "rescue" them—a reference to the pretext used for the invasion of Grenada. (Photo of the boy with the AK-47 courtesy of J. Harold Molineu; other photos by the author)

had been leaked to the U.S. press, France, Mexico, and segments of the U.S. Congress began demanding an alternative peaceful solution. Accordingly, in April the National Security Planning Group (consisting of the president and his most trusted foreign-policy advisers) adopted a top-secret but subsequently leaked planning document in which the authors stated: "We continue to have serious difficulties with U.S. public and congressional opinion, which jeopardize our ability to stay the course. International opinion, particularly in Europe and Mexico, continues to work against our policies." Later, under the category of "policy implications," these planners declared that the administration should "step up efforts to co-opt [the] negotiations issue to avoid congressionally mandated negotiations, which would work against our interests."[24]

From then on, the administration was careful to *appear* to be interested in negotiation. A roving ambassador, Richard Stone, was recruited and sent to Central America ostensibly to investigate the possibility of peace. However, as a conservative former senator from Florida and a former lobbyist for the military regime in Guatemala, Stone hardly seemed the appropriate choice for the job. Surprisingly, Stone took his formal mandate seriously. Nevertheless, in February 1984, after a long period of having been ignored and shunted aside in Reagan administration policymaking toward Central America, he resigned and was replaced by an apparently more trustworthy hawk, Harry Schlauderman.

In 1983, Colombia, Mexico, Panama, and Venezuela began their own search for a peaceful settlement—a search dubbed "the Contadora Process" after the Panamanian island on which the diplomats from the four countries had first met. Both the United States and Nicaragua expressed interest, but it was Nicaragua that, on October 15 of the same year, produced four draft peace treaties it claimed were based on the Contadora Process. Hand-delivered to the State Department by Nicaraguan Foreign Minister Miguel d'Escoto, these proposals were rejected out of hand without discussion. The Contadora Process, however, ground on, and by September 1984 the four Contadora countries, in consultation with the United States and all Central American countries, had produced the Contadora Act, a draft comprehensive peace proposal. Again, the United States had been expressing support of the Contadora Process and "officials from Honduras, Guatemala, El Salvador and Costa Rica [had] indicated their Governments would be willing to sign the treaty."[25] However, after Nicaragua surprised the world by signing unconditionally, the United States and its Central American allies did a complete reversal of position, saying that the act (which called for withdrawal of foreign military advisers, a reduction of armaments, etc.) was incomplete and that Nicaragua could not be trusted. El Salvador, Honduras, and Costa Rica, the three Central American countries most closely tied to the United States, then produced a long list of objections to the very document they had originally helped shape.

Meanwhile, representatives of the United States and Nicaragua had been holding high-level meetings in Manzanillo, Mexico. But, as one State Department official commented candidly, "I am not sure what there's left to talk about at Manzanillo. The whole point was to get the Nicaraguans to accept the Contadora proposals. Now they have, but we say we are not satisfied. I am not sure I would blame the Nicaraguans if they were confused."[26] Although the Nicaraguans were, indeed, disillusioned, they continued to try to negotiate. At a decent interval after the U.S. election of November 1984, however, even that avenue to peace was closed when the United States unilaterally broke off the Manzanillo talks.

As this material was being written in August 1985, the possibility of a peaceful solution seemed remote. Yet, while hundreds of thousands of Nicaraguans were defending or preparing to defend their country, they still exhibited a touching friendliness toward North Americans, a sense of disbelief, and an almost naive hope that somehow reason would prevail.

NOTES

1. A letter from sixty-one Nicaraguans to Major S. D. Butler, Granada, October 9, 1912. From folder 5 of the "Personal Papers" of Joseph H. Pendleton in the U.S. Marine Corps Historical Center, Washington, D.C., Naval Yard.

2. Anastasio Somoza and Jack Cox, *Nicaragua Betrayed* (Belmont, Mass.: Western Islands, 1980), pp. 77–78.

3. The shift in emphasis can be seen in a report prepared by Nelson Rockefeller after an official fact-finding visit to Latin America in 1969. Nelson A. Rockefeller, *The Rockefeller Report on the Americas* (Chicago: Quadrangle Books, 1969).

4. Though Somoza lobbying efforts were at least as extensive in the 1970s, the most detailed documentation of this type of activity pertains to the early 1960s. U.S. Congress, Senate, Committee on Foreign Relations, *Activities of Nondiplomatic Representatives of Foreign Principals in the United States*, pt. 2, hearing of March 3, 1963 (Washington, D.C.: U.S. Government Printing Office, 1963).

5. From a conversation I had with an informed source in the State Department in April 1978.

6. Richard Millett, *The Guardians of the Dynasty* (Maryknoll, N.Y.: Orbis Press, 1977), p. 252.

7. See Albert M. Colegrove, "Nicaragua: Another Cuba?" *The Nation* (July 1, 1961), pp. 6–9; and Roland Young, *The American Congress* (New York: Harper, 1958), p. 201.

8. Interview with Pedro Quintanilla, vice-minister of labor and education during the presidency of Luis Somoza, in his home in Managua on July 23, 1967.

9. For an excellent and more detailed examination of U.S. policy during the Sandinist insurrection, see William M. LeoGrande, "The Revolution in Nicaragua," *Foreign Affairs*, vol. 58, no. 1 (Fall 1979), pp. 28–50.

10. Sergio Ramírez, "What the *Sandinistas* Want," *Caribbean Review*, vol. 7, no. 3 (Summer 1979), pp. 50, 51.

11. Alejandro Bendaña, "The Foreign Policy of the Nicaraguan Revolution," in Thomas W. Walker, ed., *Nicaragua in Revolution* (New York: Praeger Publishers, 1982), p. 326.

12. Ibid.

13. For more information on Sandinista involvement in the Non-Aligned Movement see Waltraud Queiser Morales and Harry E. Vanden, "Relations with the Nonaligned Movement," in Thomas W. Walker, ed., *Nicaragua: The First Five Years* (New York: Praeger Publishers, 1985), pp. 167–184; and Robert Armstrong, "Nicaragua: Sovereignty and Non-Alignment," in *NACLA Report on the Americas*, vol. 19, no. 3 (May/June 1985), pp. 15–21.

14. From a lengthy conversation with Carlos Chamorro Coronel, chief of staff of the Ministry of Foreign Relations, in Managua, August 1980.

15. For more detailed information about this subject see Nadia Malley, "Relations with Western Europe and the Socialist International," in Walker, ed., *Nicaragua: The First Five Years*, pp. 485–498; and Robert Matthews, "The Limits of Friendship: Nicaragua and the West," *NACLA Report on the Americas*, vol. 19, no. 3 (May/June 1985), pp. 22–32.

16. Matthews, "The Limits of Friendship," pp. 29–30.

17. This is the conclusion drawn by Theodore Schwab and Harold Sims in "Relations with the Communist States," in Walker, ed., *Nicaragua: The First Five Years*, p. 161.

18. Staff Report, Subcommittee on Oversight and Evaluation, Permanent Select Committee on Intelligence, *U.S. Intelligence Performance on Central America: Achievements and Selected Instances of Concern*, September 12, 1982, mimeographed, p. 43.

19. Clifford Krauss and Robert S. Greenberger, "Despite Fears of U.S., Soviet Aid to Nicaragua Appears to Be Limited," *Wall Street Journal*, April 3, 1985, p. 1.

20. For information about the U.S.-Nicaraguan relationship see Matthews, "The Limits of Friendship"; William M. LeoGrande, "The United States and Nicaragua," in Walker, ed., *Nicaragua: The First Five Years*, pp. 425–446; and Thomas W. Walker, "Nicaraguan-U.S. Friction: The First Four Years, 1979–1983," in Kenneth M. Coleman and George C. Herring, eds., *The Central American Crisis: Sources of Conflict and The Failure of U.S. Policy* (Wilmington, Del.: Scholarly Resources, 1985), pp. 157–189.

21. Extracts from State Department and Pentagon, *Congressional Presentation Document*, Security Assistance Programs, FY 1981, as reproduced in Matthews, "The Limits of Friendship," p. 24.

22. By law, none of the $75 million was to go to health and education programs in which Cubans were involved (i.e., most health and education programs). One percent of the money was to be spent on publicly advertising the fact that the United States had given it.

23. "Nicaraguan Rebels Get Aid From White House," *New York Times* (August 8, 1985), p. 6.

24. "National Security Council Document on Policy in Central America," *New York Times* (April 7, 1983).

25. Stephen Kinzer, "Nicaraguans Say They Would Sign Proposed Treaty," *New York Times*, September 23, 1984, p. 20.

26. Philip Taubman, "U.S. Reported to Fear Sandinista Publicity Coup," *New York Times*, September 24, 1984, p. A12.

Sources in English

BOOKS

Aldaraca, Bridget; Baker, Edward; Rodríguez, Ileana; and Zimmerman, Marc, eds. *Nicaragua in Revolution: The Poets Speak/Nicaragua en Revolución: Los Poetas Hablan*. Minneapolis: Marxist Educational Press, 1980.

A bilingual collection of poems dealing with Nicaraguan history, the insurrectionary struggle, and the victory.

Americas Watch. *Human Rights in Nicaragua: Reagan, Rhetoric and Reality*. New York: Americas Watch, 1985.

Written by one of the world's major human rights monitoring organizations, this report highlights the gap between fact and rhetoric in the Reagan administration's charges concerning alleged human rights violations in Sandinista Nicaragua. Its conclusions are in conformity with evidence presented in the reports of other major human rights monitoring organizations such as Amnesty International and the Organization of American States Inter-American Commission on Human Rights (cited in note 15 of Chapter 3 of this book).

Arnove, Robert F. *Education and Revolution in Nicaragua*. New York: Praeger Publishers, forthcoming, 1986.

Based on extensive research in Nicaragua from 1980 onward, this book should provide an authoritative and valuable overview of the changing nature and role of education under the new system.

Bell, Belden, ed. *Nicaragua: An Ally Under Siege*. Washington, D.C.: Council on American Affairs, 1978.

A collection of ultraconservative articles designed to demonstrate the need for continuing aid to the Somoza system at the time that the War of Liberation was beginning.

145

Belli, Humberto. *Nicaragua: Christians Under Fire.* Garden City, Mich.: Puebla Institute, 1984.

> Produced by an exiled former editorial writer for Nicaragua's conservative daily, *La Prensa,* and distributed free of charge to members of Congress and other influential persons during the debates over aid to the *contras,* this short book is a bitter attack on alleged Sandinista violations of human rights, especially in the area of religion. It contains many inaccuracies and distortions. For alternative explanations of church-state and intra-church affairs, see the entry under O'Shaughnessy and Serra in this section. For a more dispassionate and accurate analysis of the overall human rights situation in Nicaragua, see the reports of the major international human rights monitoring organizations (cited in note 15 of Chapter 3 in this book), especially the Americas Watch report listed in this section.

Black, George. *Triumph of the People: The Sandinista Revolution in Nicaragua.* London: Zed Press, 1981.

> A solid overview of the insurrection and the first year of the new revolutionary system.

Booth, John A. *The End and the Beginning: The Nicaraguan Revolution* (2d ed.). Boulder, Colo.: Westview Press, 1985.

> One of the best overall studies of Nicaragua. Particularly useful for its examination of the historical and sociopolitical backdrop to the revolution.

Borge, Tomás, et al. *Sandinistas Speak.* New York: Pathfinder Press, 1982.

> Some translated early writings and speeches of leaders of the Sandinista revolution.

Brody, Reed. *Contra Terror in Nicaragua.* Boston: South End Press, 1985.

> A report by the former assistant attorney general of the State of New York. Based on personal investigations and over 150 interviews in Nicaragua.

Cabestrero, Teófilo. *Blood of the Innocent: Victims of the Contras' War in Nicaragua.* Maryknoll, N.Y.: Orbis Press, 1985.

> A leading specialist on the theology of liberation and a priest working closely with Nicaragua's poor, Cabestrero describes the stark human consequences of the *contra* war.

————. *Ministers of God, Ministers of the People.* Maryknoll, N.Y.: Orbis Press, 1983.

A glimpse at three Roman Catholic priests (Fernando Cardenal, Miguel D'Escoto, and Ernesto Cardenal) who served as ministers in the Sandinista government. Brief introductory sections are followed by more lengthy direct quotations from the three priests.

Cabezas, Omar. *Fire from the Mountain: The Making of a Sandinista*. New York: Crown Publishers, 1985.

An earthy, irreverent, humorous, yet tender and intimate first-person account of anti-Somoza and guerrilla activities in the late 1960s and early 1970s.

Camejo, Pedro, and Murphy, Fred, eds. *The Nicaraguan Revolution*. New York: Pathfinder Press, 1979.

Published immediately after the liberation, this short volume contains some useful speeches and interviews, as well as a translation of the Statute of Rights of Nicaraguans.

Cardenal, Ernesto. *Apocalypse and Other Poems*. New York: New Directions Publishing Corp., 1977.

A revolutionary priest and well-known poet, Cardenal became minister of culture after the liberation. This volume contains some of his translated poetry.

————. *The Gospel in Solentiname*. Four vols. Maryknoll, N.Y.: Orbis Books, 1976.

Translation of conversations concerning the meaning of the Gospel, which Cardenal conducted with his followers in the community of Solentiname.

Christian, Shirley. *Nicaragua: Revolution in the Family*. New York: Random House, 1985.

A well-written but decidedly one-sided, anti-Sandinista polemic. Christian's brief section on the 1984 election is typical both of the book as a whole and of her earlier coverage of Nicaraguan affairs for the *Miami Herald*. Although she ignores the role of Western European electoral commissions in helping design the electoral procedures, makes no mention of the favorable findings of observer teams sent by the British and Irish parliaments and the Dutch government, and overlooks the frenetically active role the United States played in cajoling, pressuring, and reportedly bribing opposition candidates not to participate, she uncritically reiterates the litany of complaints lodged against the election by an embittered privileged minority and the U.S. government.

[The CIA]. *Psychological Operations in Guerrilla Warfare.* New York: Vintage Books, 1985.

> Discovered by a member of Witness for Peace and disclosed by the U.S. media in 1984, this controversial document, prepared in 1983 by the U.S. Central Intelligence Agency, was designed to instruct the U.S.-backed *contras* fighting the Sandinistas in the techniques of guerrilla war, including assassination, misinformation, and so on. The manual is accompanied by a historical introduction by Joanne Omang (*Washington Post*) and an epilogue by Aryeh Neier (Americas Watch).

Collins, Joseph. *Nicaragua: What Difference Could a Revolution Make? Food and Farming in the New Nicaragua* (2d ed., rev.). San Francisco: Institute for Food and Development Policy, 1985.

> A beautifully written and informative study of the Sandinista revolution focusing on agrarian reform and food policy.

Cox, Isaac Joslin. *Nicaragua and the United States.* Boston: World Peace Foundation, 1928.

> A dated but nonetheless useful and scholarly examination of U.S.-Nicaraguan relations in the early twentieth century.

Crawley, Eduardo. *Nicaragua in Perspective.* New York: St. Martin's Press, 1984.

> A somewhat expanded and revised version of *Dictators Never Die: A Portrait of Nicaragua and the Somozas* (1979), this book remains an essentially journalistic effort flawed by occasional factual errors, weak analysis, and an absence of footnoting.

Diederich, Bernard. *Somoza: And the Legacy of U.S. Involvement in Central America.* New York: E. P. Dutton, 1981.

> A journalistic but nonetheless quite solid examination of the Somoza era by *Time*'s Mexico City bureau chief. Particularly rich in its coverage of events during the final years of the dictatorship.

Dixon, Marlene, ed. *On Trial, Reagan's War Against Nicaragua: Testimony of the Permanent Peoples' Tribunal.* San Francisco: Synthesis Publications, 1985.

> In the tradition of the famous Bertrand Russell Tribunals, the Permanent Peoples' Tribunal (founded in 1976) met in Brussels in October 1984 to consider and judge U.S. behavior toward Nicaragua. This volume contains the tribunal's judgment, important selected documents, and testimony from a variety of witnesses and experts.

Dixon, Marlene, and Jonas, Susanne, eds. *Nicaragua Under Siege.* San Francisco: Synthesis Publications, 1984.

A useful collection of documents and essays relating to the early stages of the Reagan administration's economic, political, and paramilitary effort to overthrow the Sandinistas.

Donahue, John M. *The Nicaraguan Revolution in Health: From Somoza to the Sandinistas.* South Hadley, Mass.: Bergen and Garvey, Publishers. Forthcoming, 1986.

Written by a U.S. scholar with considerable field experience in his subject, this will probably be the best and most comprehensive study of health in Nicaragua to date.

Eich, Dieter, and Rincón, Carlos. *The Contras: Interviews with Anti-Sandinistas.* San Francisco: Synthesis Publications, 1985.

A series of interviews of sixteen Nicaraguan *contras* by a West German and a Colombian.

Grossman, Karl. *Nicaragua: America's New Vietnam?* Sag Harbor, N.Y.: Permanent Press, 1984

An examination of some of the burning issues of the Nicaraguan revolution, based in part on interviews with actors on both sides. Though journalistic, unfootnoted, and at times superficial, this short book is generally balanced and of merit. Its coverage of the issue of alleged "religious persecution" of Christians and Jews is both accurate and important given the tremendous misinformation about that subject to which the U.S. public has been exposed.

Helms, Mary W. *Asang: Adaptations to Culture Contact in a Miskito Community.* Gainesville: University of Florida Press, 1971.

A solid ethnographic study of a Miskito community in northeastern Nicaragua.

Hirshon, Sheryl (with Judy Butler). *And Also Teach Them to Read.* Westport, Conn.: Lawrence Hill & Co., 1983.

A personal account of the activities of twenty-five rural literacy *brigadistas* during the 1980 Literacy Crusade. The author, a teacher from Oregon, served as their group leader.

Jones, Jeff, ed. *Brigadista: Harvest and War in Nicaragua.* New York: Praeger Publishers, 1985.

The eyewitness accounts of North American volunteers working in revolutionary Nicaragua.

Kamman, William. *A Search for Stability: U.S. Diplomacy Toward Nicaragua, 1925-1933.* Notre Dame: University of Notre Dame, 1968.

A thorough and useful study of an extremely important period of U.S.-Nicaraguan relations.

Kornbluh, Peter. *Nicaragua: The Price of Intervention.* Washington, D.C.: The Institute for Policy Studies, forthcoming, 1986.

Covers various aspects of U.S. intervention in Nicaragua, including the *contra* war, direct CIA activity, economic strangulation, and military encirclement.

Lappé, Frances Moore, and Collins, Joseph. *Now We Can Speak: A Journey Through the New Nicaragua.* San Francisco: Institute for Food and Development Policy, 1982.

A short but beautifully and sensitively written glimpse of the Nicaraguan revolution two years after the Triumph.

Latin American Studies Association. *The Electoral Process in Nicaragua: Domestic and International Influences (The Report of the Latin American Studies Delegation to Observe the Election of November 4, 1984).* Austin, Tex.: LASA, 1984.

A lengthy and careful study of the 1984 elections and the background conditions leading up to them. The LASA's conclusion that this had been a relatively fair and meaningful election was corroborated by delegations sent by the British and Irish parliaments and the Dutch government as well as by a number of major church and other groups. For copies of these reports, write to Reggie Norton, Washington Office on Latin America, 110 Maryland Ave., N.E., Washington, D.C. 20002 (telephone: 202/544-8045). The LASA report itself is available for $3.00 from LASA Secretariat, S. Richardson Hall, University of Texas, Austin, Texas 78712.

Lethander, Richard Walter Oscar. *The Economy of Nicaragua.* Ph.D. dissertation, Duke University, 1968.

A substantial but quite traditional examination of the Nicaraguan economic system in the mid-1960s. This and the other dissertations mentioned in this section are available for purchase in photostatic copies or microfilm from University Microfilms International, 300 N. Zeeb Road, Ann Arbor, Michigan 48106.

Levie, Alvin. *Nicaragua: The People Speak.* South Hadley, Mass.: Bergen and Garvey, Publishers, 1985.

A combination of oral history and photojournalism, this book features conversations with over eighty Nicaraguans from various walks of life and differing political viewpoints.

Macaulay, Neill. *The Sandino Affair*. Chicago: Quadrangle Books, 1967.

> A sound and scholarly study of the guerrilla war led by Augusto C. Sandino against occupying U.S. forces in the late 1920s and early 1930s.

McCuen, Gary E., ed. *The Nicaraguan Revolution: Ideas in Conflict*. Hudson, Wisconsin: Gem Publications Inc., forthcoming 1985.

Marcus, Bruce, ed. *Nicaragua: The Sandinista People's Revolution*. New York: Pathfinder Press, 1985.

> An excellent translated collection of over forty speeches by high-level revolutionary leaders in the period 1982–1984.

Miller, Valerie. *Between Struggle and Hope: The Nicaraguan Literacy Crusade*. Boulder, Colo.: Westview Press, 1985.

> An intimate and moving, yet scholarly examination of Nicaragua's 1980 Literacy Crusade by a North American scholar who served as an international adviser in that ambitious program.

Millett, Richard. *The Guardians of the Dynasty: A History of the U.S.-Created Guardia Nacional de Nicaragua and the Somoza Family*. Maryknoll, N.Y.: Orbis Books, 1977.

> A scholarly historical study of the creation of the National Guard, the rise and reign of the Somozas, and the role played in all of this by the United States.

Nietschmann, Bernard. *Between Land and Water: The Subsistence Ecology of the Miskito Indians, Eastern Nicaragua*. New York: Seminar Press, 1973.

> Like the Helms monograph, this, too, is a very sound study of a Miskito community, the turtle-fishing village of Tasbapauni.

Nolan, David. *FSLN: The Ideology of the Sandinistas and the Nicaraguan Revolution*. Coral Gables, Fla.: University of Miami Press, 1984.

> A cold war interpretation of the FSLN written without the benefit of any real field research in Nicaragua. Marred by errors in fact as well as interpretation, it was distributed gratis by the Reagan White House to all members of Congress with an accompanying note by Ambassador Faith Ryan Whittlesey stating in part that the book "provides indispensible documentation of the character of the Sandinista regime . . . which rules Nicaragua today."

O'Shaughnessy, Laura, and Serra, Luis H. *The Church and Revolution in Nicaragua*. Athens, Ohio: Papers in International Studies, Ohio University Press, 1985.

Two perspectives on the role of the church in Sandinista Nicaragua. O'Shaughnessy, a U.S. academician, finds the roots of Nicaraguan intra-church and church-state conflict in the ambiguous sociopolitical messages of the Vatican and the Latin American Bishops in the last two decades. Serra, an Argentine scholar working in popular education in revolutionary Nicaragua, relates the hierarchy's revulsion with the revolution to the church's traditional role in the reproduction of prerevolutionary, capitalist ideology.

Radell, David Richard. *An Historical Geography of Western Nicaragua: The Spheres of Influence of León, Granada, and Managua, 1519–1965.* Ph.D. dissertation, University of California, Berkeley, 1969.

A very good historical study of major regions of western Nicaragua.

Randall, Margaret. *Christians in the Nicaraguan Revolution.* Vancouver and Toronto: New Star Books, 1983.

A series of interviews with Christians supportive of the Sandinista revolution and with others describing their role.

———. *Sandino's Daughters: Testimonies of Nicaraguan Women in Struggle.* Vancouver and Toronto: New Star Books, 1981.

A series of interviews with some of the most important women in the Nicaraguan revolution.

Rosset, Peter, and Vandermeer, John. *The Nicaraguan Reader: Documents of a Revolution Under Fire.* New York: Grove Press, 1983.

A well-organized collection of short articles and other documents relating to the Nicaraguan revolution and the covert war being waged against it to late 1982.

Rudolph, James D., ed. *Nicaragua: A Country Study.* Washington, D.C.: American University, 1982.

Produced under contract with the U.S. government, this volume is in the tradition and format of the old Area Handbook series (see Ryan et al., 1970). However, it is a solid and useful study, and, remarkably, much of what is said in it contradicts the negative picture that the Reagan administration was trying to paint of Nicaragua.

Rural Women's Research Team of the Center for the Study of Agrarian Reform (CIERA). *Women's Participation in Nicaragua's Agricultural Reform.* San Francisco: Institute for Food and Development Policy, forthcoming, 1985.

Ryan, John Morris, et al. *Area Handbook on Nicaragua.* Washington, D.C.: U.S. Government Printing Office, 1970.

Though written for the U.S. government and concerned in part with "order and internal security" under the Somoza system, this study contains much valuable information about a variety of subjects pertaining to Nicaragua.

Selser, Gregorio. *Sandino*. New York: Monthly Review Press, 1981.

A translation by Cedric Belfrage of Selser's excellent two-volume Spanish-language work, *Sandino, General de hombres libres* (Buenos Aires: Editorial Triángulo, 1958). Contains many of Sandino's writings.

Somoza, Anastasio, and Cox, Jack. *Nicaragua Betrayed*. Belmont, Mass.: Western Islands, 1980.

Somoza's side of the story, of interest not so much as a reliable source of information but, rather, as a historical curiosity.

Strachan, Harry Wallace. *The Role of Business Groups in Economic Development: The Case of Nicaragua*. D.B.A. dissertation, Harvard University, 1972.

A traditional but very useful examination of the major business groups in the Nicaraguan economic system in the late 1960s.

Vilas, Carlos. *The Sandinista Revolution*. New York: Monthly Review Press, 1985.

An Argentine scholar who lived in Nicaragua from 1980 onward, Vilas provides an insightful class analysis of the insurrection and the revolutionary system that emerged after the Triumph.

Walker, Thomas W. *The Christian Democratic Movement in Nicaragua*. Tucson: University of Arizona Press, 1970.

This brief study of the Christian Democratic, or Social Christian, movement in Nicaragua examines party and related interest-group organization and activity during the heyday of the Christian Democratic opposition in the 1960s.

————, ed. *Nicaragua: The First Five Years*. New York: Praeger Publishers, 1985.

A product of the field research of over thirty scholars, this book systematically examines the Nicaraguan Revolution through its first half-decade in power. Its twenty-five chapters focus on a variety of topics under four main headings: Power and Interests, Economic Policy, Social Policy, and the International Dimension. An epilogue contains a condensed version of the LASA report on the 1984 elections.

————, ed. *Nicaragua in Revolution*. New York: Praeger Publishers, 1982.

Similar in concept to *Nicaragua: The First Five Years*, this earlier volume concentrates on the first year and a half of revolutionary rule. In addition, it features a three-chapter section dealing with the insurrection.

———, ed. *Reagan vs. the Sandinistas: The Undeclared War on Nicaragua.* Boulder, Colo.: Westview Press, forthcoming.

Also utilizing a team approach, this book is designed to provide a comprehensive examination of the most massive action, short of direct U.S. invasion, ever mounted by the United States against a foreign government. In addition to dealing with obvious topics such as the *contra* invasion, military encirclement, and economic destabilization, it examines disinformation, the "patriotic agenda" in the U.S. media, radio-TV penetration of Nicaragua, and the implications of Reagan's Nicaragua policy for international law and world order.

Walker, (General) William. *The War in Nicaragua.* Tucson: University of Arizona Press, 1985.

A personal account of "the first American invasion of Central America," by William Walker, the U.S. adventurer who briefly imposed himself as president of Nicaragua in the 1850s.

Weber, Henri. *Nicaragua: The Sandinista Revolution.* London: Verso Editions, 1981.

A worthwhile examination of the insurrection and evaluation of the first year of revolutionary rule.

Wheelock Román, Jaime. *Nicaragua: The Great Challenge.* Managua: Alternative Views, 1984.

An extensive interview by Marta Harnecker, with Jaime Wheelock, minister of agrarian reform and member of the Sandinista Directorate.

Women's International Resource Exchange. *Nicaraguan Women: Unlearning the Alphabet of Submission.* New York: WIRE, 1985.

A short collection of essays and articles dealing with women in Nicaragua.

Zimmerman, Mark, ed. *Nicaragua in Reconstruction and at War: The People Speak.* Minneapolis: Marxist Educational Press, 1985.

A collage of chronology, analysis, and poetry portraying the insurrection, reconstruction, and U.S. intervention.

Zwerling, Philip, and Martin, Connie. *Nicaragua: A New Kind of Revolution.* Westport, CT: Lawrence Hill, 1985.

A series of conversations with dozens of people from all levels of leadership in the Nicaraguan revolution.

PERIODICALS

Clearly the most useful and scholarly English language periodical devoted to Nicaragua is *Envío* (English Edition). Published monthly by the Instituto Histórico Centroamericano in Managua, it is reproduced and distributed in the United States ($35.00 per subscription) by the Central American Historical Institute, Intercultural Center, Room 307, Georgetown University, Washington, D.C. 20057.

Also of interest are:

1. *Barricada Internacional*. An English language weekly version of the official FSLN party organ. Annual subscription: $24.00 (U.S.), from *Barricada Internacional*, Apartado 579, Managua, Nicaragua.

2. *LASA-NICA Scholars News*. A short monthly newsletter of the Latin American Studies Association's Task Force on Scholarly Relations with Nicaragua. Useful mainly for scholars interested in doing research in, or knowing about, scholarly activities concerning Nicaragua. Annual subscription: $8.00, from the Latin American Studies Association, Sid Richardson Hall, Unit 1, The University of Texas, Austin, Texas 78712.

3. *Nicaraguan Perspectives*. A quarterly magazine. Annual subscription: $12.00, from Nicaraguan Information Center, P.O. Box 1004, Berkeley, California 94704.

4. *Update*. News updates on key Nicaraguan issues produced and mailed in packets of two to three monthly for an annual charge of $30.00 by the U.S. distributors of *Envío*.

Index

Abscam, 127
Academic titles, 85
Accessory Transit Company, 58
Afghanistan, 132
AFL-CIO (American Federation of
  Labor-Congress of Industrial
  Organizations). *See*
  Confederation of Labor Unity
Agency for International
  Development (AID), U.S., 31–
  32, 34
Agricultural machinery, 62, 72
Agriculture. *See individual crops;
  under* Nicaragua
Agüero, Fernando, 30, 31. *See also*
  Somoza-Agüero pact
AID. *See* Agency for International
  Development
Alemán-Bolaños, Gustavo, 76
Algeria, 135
Alliance for Progress (1961), 29,
  62, 63, 102, 126, 127
American Federation of Labor-
  Congress of Industrial
  Organizations (AFL-CIO). *See*
  Confederation of Labor Unity
Amnesty International, 32
AMNLAE. *See* Luisa Amanda
  Espinosa Association of
  Nicaraguan Women
AMPRONAC. *See* Association of
  Women Confronting the
  National Problem
Anti-Sandinista paramilitary
  training camps (U.S.), 46

Arbenz, Jacobo, 27
Arce, Bayardo, 105(port.), 106
Argentina, 38, 68
Argüello, Santiago, 76
Art, 77, 79, 112–113(illus.)
Association of Women Confronting
  the National Problem
  (AMPRONAC), 84
ASTC. *See* Sandinista Association
  of Cultural Workers
ATC. *See* Rural Workers'
  Association
Atlantic region, 82, 83, 125
Austria, 68, 133
Aztec civilization, 57

Banamérica Group, 64, 65
"Banana republic" economy, 60–61
Bananas, 16, 62, 127
Banco Central, 28, 63, 65
Banco Centroamericano, 65
Banco de América, 64
Banco Nacional, 65
Banco Nicaragüense (BANIC), 64–
  65
BANIC. *See* Banco Nicaragüense
Banking system, 64–65, 68, 69
Barcenas Meneses-Esguerra Treaty
  (1928), 125
Basic human needs, 66
Bay of Pigs invasion (1961), 126
Beans, 57, 78, 91
Beef, 62, 91
Beer, 78
Billboards, 112–113(illus.)

Bluefields 17, 18
Bolivia, 56
Borge, Tomás, 40, 77, 105(port.)
Bourgeoisie, 41
Brandt, Willy, 133
Brazil, 55, 68, 93, 128
Breast feeding campaign, 113(illus.)
Broad Opposition Front (FAO), 36, 37
Bryan-Chamorro Treaty (1916), 20, 124, 125
Bunker, El, 36
Bureaucracy, 61
Butler, Smedley D., 19

Cabestrero, Teófilo, 108(port.)
Cacao, 57, 78
Cacique (chief), 6
California, 46, 58
Canada, 68
Capital flight, 68
Capital-intensive industry, 62
Capitalism, 55
Cardenal, Ernesto, 77
Cardenal, Fernando, 96
Caribbean lowlands, 2
Carrión, Luis, 105(port.)
Cartel schemes, 127
Carter, Jimmy, 33, 36, 44, 129–130
Cassava, 57, 78
Castorseed, 72
Castro, Andrés, 6
Castro, Fidel, 62, 134
Catholic Church, 2, 12, 32, 43. See also Christian Base Communities; under Sandinist Front of National Liberation
Catholic intellectuals, 101
Cattle, 3, 12, 57, 60, 62
CDCs. See Civil Defense Committees
CDRS. See Ramiro Sacasa Democratic Coordinating Committee
CDSs. See Sandinista Defense Committees

Censorship, 100, 118. See also Precensorship
Census, 16
Central America, 58. See also individual countries
Central American Common Market (1960), 63
Central American Court of Justice, 19, 20–21
Central American Defense Council (CONDECA), 126
Central American Federation, 13
Central American Institute of Business Administration (INCAE), 63
Central highlands, 2, 60
Central Intelligence Agency (CIA), 27, 44, 46, 48, 51, 71, 83, 91, 126, 137
Chamorro, Diego Manuel, 20
Chamorro, Emiliano, 20
Chamorro, Fernando, 36
Chamorro, Pedro Joaquín (19th century president of Nicaragua), 59
Chamorro, Pedro Joaquín (20th century journalist), 33, 34–35, 76
Chamorro, Violeta, 47
Chamorro family, 45
Chase Manhattan Bank, 65
Chicha, 78
Chile, 55
Chili, 57, 78
Chinandega, 37
Christian Base Communities (CEBs), 41–42
Christmas bonuses, 89
CIA. See Central Intelligence Agency
Circus, 79
Civil Defense Committees (CDCs), 90, 93
Class polarization, 42, 45, 46
Clayton-Bulwer Treaty (1850), 13
Cleveland, Grover, 17

Club Terraza (Managua), 69
Coffee, 2, 3, 15, 16, 58–59, 60, 61, 62, 78
 boom (late 1800s), 58
 cartel scheme, 127
 harvest, 59
Collective bargaining, 102
Colombia, 18, 55, 125, 140
Columbia University. *See* María Moors Cabot Prize
Communes, 59, 60
Communists. *See* Nicaraguan Communist party; Nicaraguan Socialist party
Compa, 85
Compañero, 85
Compita, 85
Comte, Auguste, 16
CONDECA. *See* Central American Defense Council
Confederation of Labor Unity (CUS), 102, 114
Conference of Amapala (1895), 17
Conquistadores, 57
Conservative party. *See* Conservatives
Conservatives, 13, 14, 15, 18, 19, 20, 21, 28, 30–31, 60, 64, 100, 101, 105, 124, 125
 rebellion (1909), 61
Constitutional Liberal party (PLC), 114
Consumers, 55–56
Contadora Act peace proposal (1984), 140–141
Contadora Process, 140
Contras, 46, 47, 48, 51, 81, 83, 88, 91, 106, 114, 135, 137, 138–139(illus.), 140
 Honduran bases, 46, 83, 87, 136
 social and economic infrastructural damage, 69, 71, 72, 97
 See also Nicaraguan Democratic Forces
Cooking oil, 91

Cooperatives, 89, 109
Coordinadora, la. See Ramiro Sacasa Democratic Coordinating Committee
COPPPAL. *See* Permanent Conference of Political Parties of Latin America
Cordilleras, 1
Córdoba Rivas, Rafael, 115
Corn, 57, 91
 as beverage, 78–79
 masa (dough), 78
 See also Tortillas
Corn Islands. *See* Great and Little Corn Islands
Coronel Urtecho, José, 77
Corruption, 63, 64, 66, 72, 100, 103, 127
COSEP. *See* Superior Council of Private Enterprise
Costa Rica, 20, 140, 141
Costeños, 82, 83
Cottage industry, 58
Cotton, 62, 70(illus.), 133
Council of State, 45, 46, 82, 84, 105, 106, 116
Counterinsurgency, 136
Counterrevolutionaries, 87–88. *See also Contras*
Country clubs, 85
Credit, 89
Crime, 109
Cruz, Arturo, 52, 117
CST. *See* Sandinista Workers Central
CTN. *See* Social Christian Confederation of Workers of Nicaragua
Cuadra, Pablo Antonio, 76
Cuba, 62, 68, 93, 126, 132, 134
Cuisine, 78–79
Culture, 56, 75–79. *See also* Art; Language; Literature; Music
CUS. *See* Confederation of Labor Unity

Darío, Rubén, 76

Day-care centers, 89, 91
Debayle, Luis Manuel, 103
Debayle, Salvadora, 25
Debt peonage, 59
Decapitalization, 86
Decentralization, 51, 107
Delegates of the Word, 41, 42,
    108(port.)
Delinquent minors, 91
Democratic Armed Forces (FAD),
    86
Democratic Conservative party
    (PCD), 114, 115, 117, 119
Denmark, 68, 133
Dependency, 3, 6, 7. *See also*
    Dependent capitalism
Dependent capitalism, 55, 56, 60–
    66, 79
Dependent economic development,
    126
D'Escoto, Miguel, 140
Destabilization, 45, 48, 69, 72, 130
Development, 63, 126. *See also*
    under Nicaragua
Díaz, Adolfo, 19, 20
Díaz, Porfirio, 62
Dictatorship, 55
Dignidad, 75
Diriamba, 37
Diriangén, 6, 10
Disease, 57, 80, 90, 97
Disinformation, 42
Displaced persons, 91, 92
DN. *See* Sandinista Directorate
Dominican Republic, 55, 126
Drought (1982), 48, 69

ECOSOC. *See* United Nations
    Economic and Social Council
Education, 7, 29, 49, 81, 89, 90,
    97
    adult, 97
    See also Literacy Crusade
Eggs, 91
Electoral Law (1984), 51, 116, 118
El Retiro, 79
El Salvador, 17, 20, 137, 140, 141

election (1984), 118
human rights, 48
population density, 56
press, 51
See also Soccer War
Embroidered clothing, 77
ENABAS. *See* National Foodstuffs
    Enterprise
English (language), 97
Episcopal Conference of Nicaragua,
    33
Estelí, 37, 39

FAD. *See* Democratic Armed Forces
FAO. *See* Broad Opposition Front
Family planning program (1967),
    80
FDN. *See* Nicaraguan Democratic
    Forces
Fertilizer, 62
Feudal society, 57
Final Offensive (1979), 109
First National Bank of Boston, 64
Flood (1982), 48, 69, 91
Flor de Caña (rum), 79
Florida, 45, 46
Fonseca, Gulf of, 20
Fonseca Amador, Carlos, 6, 40, 93,
    112(port.)
Food, 87, 90
    consumption, 91
    prices, 89, 91, 97
    production, 69, 91
    subsidies, 49, 97
    See also Cuisine
Foreign exchange, 48, 69
Foreign investment, 63
Forest products, 57
FPR. *See* Revolutionary Patriotic
    Front
France, 49, 134, 135, 140
Freire, Paulo, 93, 96
FSLN. *See* Sandinist Front of
    National Liberation
Fund to Combat Unemployment,
    88

Gallo pinto (bean and rice dish), 78
Garlic, 72
GDP. *See* Gross domestic product
General Confederation of Labor, 102
General Statistics Office, 16
Geothermal energy, 56
Ginger, 72
GNP. *See* Gross national product
Godoy, Virgilio, 117
Gold, 6, 10, 12, 13, 16, 56, 57
Governing Junta of National Reconstruction (JGRN), 45, 105, 106, 115, 131, 133
Granada, 11–12, 13, 82
Grassroots organizations, 40–42, 43, 44, 49, 107–109
Great and Little Corn Islands, 20
Great Britain, 106, 117. *See also under* Nicaragua
Gross domestic product (GDP), 68
Gross national product (GNP), 63. *See also under* Nicaragua
"Guarantees of inexpropriability," 69
Guardia Nacional. *See* National Guard
Guatemala, 27, 48, 126, 140
Guerrilla foci, 41, 126. *See also* Nicaragua, guerrilla action
Guinea-Bissau, 93

Hacienda (ranch), 60
Handicrafts, 77, 79
Hardwoods, 56
Harvard University School of Business Administration, 63
Health care, 7, 49, 81, 89, 90, 97
Health crusade, 47
Hernández de Córdoba, Francisco, 10, 11
Hides, 57
Highways, 82
Honduran-Nicaraguan border patrol, 137
Honduras, 17, 19, 137, 140, 141

and U.S., 48, 136, 137
See also Contras, Honduran bases; Soccer War
House Committee on Intelligence (U.S.), 47, 135
House Subcommittee on International Relations (U.S.), 32
Housing, 7, 28, 29, 49, 89, 90, 91–92, 97
Hüeck, Cornelio, 33
Huertas, 58
Hughes, Howard, 128
Human rights, 48, 77, 129, 130. *See also under* Sandinist Front of National Liberation; Somoza Debayle, Anastasio
Hydroelectric energy, 56

IDB. *See* Inter-American Development Bank
IMF. *See* International Monetary Fund
Immaculate Conception of Mary festivities, 77
INCAE. *See* Central American Institute of Business Administration
Income
 distribution, 3, 56
 national, 56
 redistribution, 60
Independent Liberal party (PLI), 101, 114, 115, 117, 119
Industrialization, 63
Infant diarrhea, 90
Infant mortality, 90
Inflation, 48
Infrastructure, 82. *See also Contras,* social and economic infrastructural damage
Inoculation campaigns, 90
INPRHU. *See* Institute for Human Promotion
Insecticides, 62
INSSBI. *See* Nicaraguan Social Security and Welfare Institute

162

INDEX

Institute for Human Promotion
(INPRHU), 102
Institute of National Development,
28
Instituto de Oriente, 16
Instituto Nacional de Oriente, 25
Inter-American Development Bank
(IDB), 46, 48, 69
Interest associations, 64–65, 104,
105, 106
Internal waterways, 2, 56
International Committee for the
Defense of the Nicaraguan
Revolution, 133
International Monetary Fund
(IMF), 38
International relief funds, 31–32,
64, 127
Iran, 133
Ireland, 117
Irrigation, 62
Israel, 38
Italy, 134
Iturbide, Agustín de, 13

Japan, 18
Jesús Marchena (Chamorro), 77
JGRN. *See* Governing Junta of
National Reconstruction
Jinotepe, 37
JMRs. *See* Municipal Juntas for
Reconstruction
JS-19. *See* Sandinista Youth
Judicial system, 106

Kissinger, Henry, 129
Kissinger Commission, 71, 97
Korean airliner shooting, 132
Korean War, 62

Labor, 55, 62
mobilization, 42
movement, 101, 102. *See also*
Unions
physical, 85
seasonal, 59

shortage, 59, 68, 81. *See also*
Unemployment
trained, 68
Láinez, Francisco ("Ché"), 63, 64
Land
distribution, 89, 109
ownership, 59, 62, 65, 90, 92
renting of, 69
speculation, 92
Langer, William, 128
Language, 2, 9, 11, 14, 56, 75–76,
82, 85, 97
LASA. *See* Latin American Studies
Association
Latin America, 41, 42, 55–56, 127.
See also individual countries
Latin American Bishops
Conference (1968), 41
Latin American Studies Association
(LASA), 52, 117, 118
Leatherwork, 77
Lebanon, 132
Leimos massacre, 83
Lenin, V. I., 42
León, 11, 12, 13, 37, 40, 82
Ley de Amparo (Law of Protection),
68–69
Liberal democracy, 55
Liberal International, 132
Liberal party. *See* Liberals
Liberals, 13, 14, 15, 18, 20, 21, 22,
29, 31, 33, 61, 100, 101, 105,
124, 125, 130
Libya, 68, 133
Literacy Crusade (1980), 45, 82,
86, 92–97, 109, 115
Literature, 76–77, 79
Livestock, 56. *See also* Cattle
López Pérez, Rigoberto, 28
Louisiana State University, 28
Lower classes, 56, 85
Luisa Amanda Espinosa
Association of Nicaraguan
Women (AMNLAE), 84, 93,
107
Luxury goods, 85

Machismo, 84–85
Madriz, José, 18
Malaria, 90
Malnutrition, 91
Managua, 15, 31, 36, 37, 51, 79, 89, 127
  capital (1852), 82
Managua, Lake, 2
Managua, Treaty of (1860), 17
Mangoes, 72
Manzanillo (Mexico) meeting, 141
MAP-ML. *See* Marxist-Leninist Popular Action Movement
María Moors Cabot Prize, 35
Marines, U.S., 19, 21, 23
Marx, Karl, 42
Marxism. *See* Sandinist Front of National Liberation, as Marxist
Marxism-Leninism, 42, 43, 71
Marxist Independent General Confederation of Labor, 102
Marxist-Leninist Popular Action Movement (MAP-ML), 114, 115, 119
Masa. See under Corn
Masaya, 35, 37
Mass mobilization, 41, 42
Mass organizations, 43
Matagalpa, 37
Mayan civilization, 57
Mayorga, Silvio, 40
MDN. *See* Nicaraguan Democratic Movement
Meat, 57, 62
Medellín (Colombia), 41, 88
Mejía Godoy, Carlos, 77
Melons, 72
Meso-American languages, 9
Mestizo, 2, 11
Mexico, 48, 62, 68, 93, 140
Miami (Fla.), 40, 45
  Heart Institute, 33
Microparties, 86, 88, 101
Middle class, 42, 56, 61, 68, 91
Middle sector, 84, 85, 89
Military draft (1983), 114

Military rule, 55
Milk, 91
Minerals, 56
Minifaldas. See Technocrats
Mining of harbors (1984), 48, 71
"Miniskirts." *See* Technocrats
Ministry of Culture, 79, 115
Ministry of Defense, 105
Ministry of Foreign Affairs, 115, 132
Ministry of Housing and Human Settlements (MINVAH), 91
Ministry of the Interior, 46, 105
MINVAH. *See* Ministry of Housing and Human Settlements
Miskito (language), 97
Miskito Coast, 13, 47
Miskito Indians, 13, 17, 47, 82, 83, 97–98(n6)
Misurasata (Indian organization), 82
Mixed economy, 44, 72
Mobs. *See Turbas*
Modernism (literary movement), 76
Moncada, José María, 21
Monimbó (Masaya), 35–36
Monroe Doctrine (1823), 17
Morales, Armando, 77
Mountain leprosy, 90
Movement of Non-Aligned Countries, 132
Movie industry, 79
Municipal Juntas for Reconstruction (JMRs), 107
Murals, 79, 112(illus.)
Museums, 79
Music, 76, 77

Nacatamal, 78
National Archives and Museum, 16
National Assembly, 52, 105, 119
National Bank, 21
National Bipartisan Commission on Central America. *See* Kissinger Commission
National Consultation process, 120
National Emergency Committee, 31

National Foodstuffs Enterprise
(ENABAS), 91
National Guard, 21, 23, 25, 26, 27,
28, 29, 30, 31, 32, 33, 34, 35,
37, 39, 40, 41, 43, 63, 81, 83,
84, 86, 100, 106, 109, 125,
128, 129, 130
National Housing Institute, 28
Nationalism, 6
Nationalization. *See under*
Nicaragua
National Legislative Palace
(Managua), 36–37
National Literacy Crusade. *See*
Literacy Crusade
National Palace operation (1978),
130
National School of Fine Arts
(Managua), 77
National Security Council (U.S.),
130
National Security Planning Group
(U.S.), 140
National Union of (Small) Farmers
and Cattlemen (UNAG), 107,
108(illus.)
Neopositivism, 62
Netherlands, 117
New Sandinist Economy, 66–67,
68, 69, 71–72
Nicaragua
agrarian reform, 29, 89–90, 102
agriculture, 2, 9, 56, 57, 58, 59–
60, 62, 69, 72, 89. *See also*
individual crops
birth control, 80
birth rate, 80, 81
borders, 43, 75
canal proposal, 61, 124
capital. *See* Managua
in Central American Federation
(1823), 13
class structure, 42, 56, 61, 81,
84–88, 106. *See also* Class
polarization
climate, 1, 2, 56

coasts, 56, 62, 82, 83
and Colombia, 125
colonial period (1522–1822), 10–
12, 57–58, 82
conservative period (1857–1893),
15
constitution, 16, 30, 31, 99, 100.
See also under Sandinist Front
of National Liberation
death rate, 80, 90
development, 28, 29, 30, 56, 61,
63–64
earthquake (1972), 31, 64, 127,
129
economic aid to, 127–128. *See*
also under Sandinist Front of
National Liberation
economic cycles, 60–61, 62
economic potential, 56, 72
economy, 28, 57–66, 126–127.
See also under Sandinist Front
of National Liberation
elites, 3, 6, 7, 12, 15, 42, 58, 59,
60, 62, 84–85, 87(illus.), 102,
124, 125, 130
exports, 3, 6, 7, 16, 28, 48, 57,
58, 60, 61, 62, 69, 72, 91
foreign aid to, 66
foreign debt, 44, 48, 67, 69, 72
GDP, 68, 69, 71, 72
geography, 1–2
Germans in, 65
GNP, 3, 56
government, 99–103. *See also*
under Sandinist Front of
National Liberation
and Great Britain, 6, 12, 13, 14–
15, 17, 18, 58, 82, 123
guerrilla action, 22, 32, 34. *See*
also Sandinist Front of
National Liberation, guerrilla
warfare
illiteracy rate (1983), 97
imports, 48, 69
independence (1838), 13, 58, 123

independence day (September 14), 15
Indians, 2, 9-11, 12, 13, 15, 57, 59, 76, 82. *See also* Miskito Indians
life expectancy in, 3, 90
literacy, 7. *See also* Literacy Crusade
median age, 80
in Mexican Empire (1822), 13
military aid to, 128
National Congress, 30
nationalization in, 7, 22, 68, 92
natural resources, 1, 56
people of, 2-3, 4-5(illus.), 9, 11, 81. *See also* Culture
population, 1, 2, 80, 123
population density, 56
population/land ratio, 56
pre-Columbian period, 9-10, 57, 82
religion, 2, 12, 75, 77-78, 82. *See also* Catholic Church
revolution (1979), 1, 6-7, 81. *See also* Sandinist Front of National Liberation
rural, 80, 81, 89, 101-102
size, 1, 56
and Spain, 3, 6, 10, 57-58
strikes, 37
urban, 88, 89. *See also* Urbanization
and U.S., 6, 13-15, 17-19, 20-21, 22, 23, 27-28, 33, 38, 61, 64, 123, 124-130. *See also* Alliance for Progress; *under* Sandinist Front of National Liberation
and U.S. military bases in, 13, 126
war damages, 69, 72, 89, 91, 131
See also Dependency
Nicaragua, Lake, 2, 12
Nicaraguan Communist party (PCN), 114, 115, 119

Nicaraguan Democratic Forces (FDN), 114
Nicaraguan Democratic Movement (MDN), 46
Nicaraguan Housing Bank, 34
Nicaraguan Social Christian party (PSCN), 101, 114
Nicaraguan Socialist party (PSN), 40, 101, 114, 115, 119
and Soviet Union, 41
Nicaraguan Social Security and Welfare Institute (INSSBI), 90
Nicaragüense, El (Cuadra), 76
Nicarao, 10
Nicaráuac (journal), 79
1980 Program for Economic Reactivation in Benefit of the People, The, 55
Niquinohomo, 19
Nixon, Richard, 128
Nonalignment, 132
Nuñez, Carlos, 105(port.)

OAS. *See* Organization of American States
Obando y Bravo, Miguel, 115
Oil-storage facilities destruction (1983), 48, 71
Oil supplies, 48
Olympics (1984), 132
Onions, 72
Operation Pigpen, 36-37, 41
Operation Red Christmas, 84
Organization of American States (OAS), 38, 39, 130
Orphans, 91
Ortega Saavedra, Daniel, 52, 105(port.), 119, 133
Ortega Saavedra, Humberto, 105(port.)
Oversocialization (Cuba), 68

"Pact of the generals," 28
Panama, 15, 18, 37, 125, 140
Panama Canal, 124
Zone, 128, 129

Pancasán disaster (1967), 41
Paraguay, 120(n2)
Pastora, Edén, 36
PCD. *See* Democratic Conservative party
PCN. *See* Nicaraguan Communist party
"Peaceful coexistence," 41
Peace of Tipitapa (1927), 125
Peanuts, 72
Peasants, 59, 60, 69, 89–90, 129
  farms. *See* Huertas
  independent, 59
  mobilization, 42, 102
  and politics, 101
People's Republic of China (PRC), 133
Pérez Jiménez, Marcos, 55
Permanent Conference of Political Parties of Latin America (COPPPAL), 132
Peru, 11, 68
Pez Y La Serpiente, El (literary journal), 76
Pierce School of Business Administration (Philadelphia), 25
Piñata, la, 79
Pine forests, 56
Pirates, 6, 12, 58, 82
Plantain, 59
Plantation commissaries, 59
Plasmaféresis de Nicaragua (company), 34, 66
PLC. *See* Constitutional Liberal party
PLI. *See* Independent Liberal party
Polio, 90
Political literacy, 96
Political participation, 104, 109, 120
Political parties, 100–101, 106, 114–115
  Law (1983), 51, 116
  See also Microparties
Political pluralism, 44, 46

Political prisoners, 47
Political socialization, 109, 114
Popular Anti-Somocista Tribunals (TPAs), 106
Popular Health Days, 90
Popular Social Christian party (PPSC), 101, 114, 115, 119
Potatoes, 78
Pottery, 77
Poultry, 91
Poverty, 80
PPSC. *See* Popular Social Christian party
PRC. *See* People's Republic of China
Precensorship, 51
Prensa, La (Managua), 33, 45, 46, 47, 51, 76, 86, 88, 119
Press, freedom of the, 88, 129–130
Press law, 47
Preventive detention, 51
Private sector, 42, 43, 45, 68, 69, 86, 89, 93, 116, 134
"Progressive urbanizations," 92
Proletarian Tendency (TP), 41
Prolonged Popular War (GPP), 41
Property, 68–69
  confiscation, 44–45, 68, 85, 102
Prostitution, 84, 91
Protestants, 82, 107
Providencia Island, 125
PSCN. *See* Nicaraguan Social Christian party
PSD. *See* Social Democratic party
PSN. *See* Nicaraguan Socialist party
Public sector, 68
Public works projects, 88–89
Purísima, La festivities, 77–78

Quainton, Anthony, 47

Radio stations, 77, 119
Railroads, 82
Ramírez, Sergio, 52, 77, 119, 131

Ramiro Sacasa Democratic Coordinating Committee (CDRS), 115, 117
Rape, 84
Reagan, Ronald, 42, 44, 45, 46, 51, 52, 67–68, 83, 86, 114, 116, 134, 137
Rebozo, Bebe, 128
Regional economic integration, 63
Regionalism, 81–83
Regions, 51, 107
Regulations of Syndical Associations, 102
Rent reduction and controls, 92
República Mayor (Greater Republic), 17
Revolutionary Patriotic Front (FPR), 115
Rice, 78, 91
Richter 7 (Chamorro), 76–77
Río Coco, 23, 47, 83
Rivas, Patricio, 14
Rivers, 56
Roosevelt, Franklin Delano, 126
Ruíz, Henry, 105(port.)
Rum, 79
Rural proletariat, 59, 62, 89, 101–102
Rural-urban migration, 81
Rural Workers' Association (ATC), 102, 107, 109

Sacasa, Juan B., 21, 27
Sacasa, Roberto, 15
Salazar, Jorge, 46
Salsa de chile, 78
San Andrés Island, 125
Sandinista Army, *See* Sandinist Popular Army
Sandinista Association of Cultural Workers (ASTC), 79
Sandinista Defense Committees (CDSs), 46, 107, 109
Sandinista Directorate (DN), 43, 104, 105, 116, 131
Sandinista Militias, 47, 49, 84, 114, 135

Sandinista Workers Central (CST), 107
Sandinista Youth (JS-19), 107
Sandinist Front of National Liberation (FSLN) (1961), 6, 22, 30, 32, 34, 35, 36–37, 38–41, 130
    air force, 135
    armed forces, 44, 109–111, 114, 134, 135. *See also* Sandinista Army; Sandinista Militias
    arms, 49, 109–110, 134, 135, 137
    battle hymn, 136–137
    and Catholic Church, 43, 46, 88, 93, 96, 115
    constitution, 119–120
    and Cuba, 93, 134, 136
    and death penalty, 45, 106
    defense spending, 49, 72, 97
    economic aid to, 44, 67–68, 69, 134, 136
    economic plan, 55. *See also* New Sandinist Economy
    and economy, 44, 45, 46, 47, 48–49, 69, 71–72, 86, 88, 116
    election observers, 117–118
    and elections, 51–52, 115, 116–119
    factions, 41, 104
    and foreign debt, 67, 69, 72, 88, 103
    foreign policy, 44, 67, 132–136
    government (1979), 42, 43, 44, 51, 107, 116. *See also* Council of State; Governing Junta of National Reconstruction; Judicial system; National Assembly; Sandinista Directorate
    guerrilla warfare, 41, 109, 110
    and Honduras, 137
    and human rights, 43, 45, 46, 47–48, 51, 53–54(n15)
    and labor movement, 102
    as Marxist, 40, 42, 43, 136

military aid to, 39, 44, 47, 49,
    134–135
opposition to, 46, 86, 88, 105,
    114, 115–116, 119. *See also*
    Contras
paving-block barricades, 39
and Socialist Bloc, 43, 44, 47,
    49, 67, 68, 133, 134, 135, 136
social programs, 43, 44, 45, 47,
    49, 88–97
and Soviet Union, 43, 48, 132,
    135
strategy, 41, 43, 44, 45, 47, 49
supporters of, 105, 106, 110, 115
and Third World, 67, 132
trade policy, 67, 72, 133
and UN, 132
and U.S., 42–43, 44, 45–46, 47,
    48, 49, 51, 52, 67–68, 69, 72,
    114, 117, 118, 131–133, 134,
    135, 136–137, 140–141. *See*
    also Central Intelligence
    Agency; Destabilization
and U.S. invasion possibility, 135
and U.S. trade, 67, 68, 79, 134
and Western Europe, 68, 117,
    120, 133–134, 135, 137
women in, 84
Sandinist National Police, 84
Sandinist Popular Army, 44, 46,
    47, 84, 114
Sandinist Popular Militias. *See*
    Sandinista Militias
Sandino, Augusto César, 6, 20, 21–
    23, 26, 41, 83, 112(port.), 125,
    132
San Juan River, 2, 12, 13
Schick Gutiérrez, René, 29
Schlauderman, Harry, 140
Seafood, 62
"Secret" ballot, 100
Self-determination, 61, 132
Selva, Salomón de la, 76
Sesame seed, 72
Shelton, Turner, 30, 128–129
Shipbuilding, 57

SI. *See* Socialist International
Silver, 56
Slash-and-burn agriculture, 2, 9
Slaves, 3, 11, 14, 57, 82
Soccer War (1969), 63
Social Christian Confederation of
    Workers of Nicaragua (CTN),
    102, 114
Social Democratic party (PSD), 114
Social Democrats of West Europe.
    See Socialist International
Socialist Bloc, 132. *See also under*
    Sandinist Front of National
    Liberation
Socialist International (SI), 117,
    132, 133
Social revolution, 85–86
Social security, 90–91
"*Somocismo* without Somoza," 130
Somocistas, 106
Somoza Debayle, Anastasio, 6, 28,
    29, 30, 103(port.), 128
    death, 120(n2)
    and elections, 100, 101
    and foreign debt, 67, 69
    and human rights, 32–33, 36,
        77, 129, 130
    as president (1967–1972), 30–31,
        129
    as president (1974–1979), 31–35,
        36, 38, 40, 41, 42, 63, 79, 80,
        100–101
    and relief funds, 31–32, 64, 127
    and U.S., 125–127, 136
Somoza Debayle, Luis, 28–29, 30,
    40, 64, 128
    as president (1957–1963), 29–30,
        100, 101
Somoza García, Anastasio
    ("Tacho"), 23, 25, 26, 27, 40,
    61
    assassinated (1956), 128
    as president (1937–1956), 27–28,
        63
    and U.S., 125, 126
    wealth, 28, 65

Somoza Portocarrero, Anastasio, III, 36, 37
Somosa-Agüero pact (1971), 129
Somoza family, 6, 23, 25, 27, 62, 63, 72, 85
wealth, 65–66, 68, 103
Somosa Lobby, 127
Southwest (U.S.), 46
Soviet Union, 41, 132. *See also under* Sandinist Front of National Liberation
Spain. *See under* Nicaragua
Spanish-American War (1898), 17
Spare parts, 72
Special tribunals, 106
Special Zones, 51, 107
Spencer, Herbert, 16
Squatter farmers, 59
Stalinism, 41
State farms, 89, 109
State monopoly, 69
State of prewar emergency (1982), 51
Stone, Richard, 140
Students, 42, 101
Subsidy Laws (1879, 1889), 60
Subsistence farming, 59, 60
Sugar, 48, 62
Superior Council of Private Enterprise (COSEP), 46, 88, 115–116
Surrogate invasion, 45
Sweden, 68, 118, 133

Taft, William Howard, 16
Taiwan, 133
Tallow, 57
Tamales, 78
Taxes, 85, 88
Technocrats, 30, 61, 63, 100
Technology, 61, 63
Television, 79, 119
Terceristas, 41
Theberge, James, 33
Third Force. *See* Terceristas
Third World. *See under* Sandinist Front of National Liberation

Tiempo muerto (unemployment between harvests), 59
Timber, 3, 12, 16, 56, 62
Tirado López, Victor, 105(port.)
Tobacco, 57
Tomatoes, 78
Tortillas, 78
Toys, 79
TPAs. *See* Popular Anti-Somocista Tribunals
Trade embargo (1985), 67, 68, 79, 134
Transportation, 56, 58, 61
Trujillo, Rafael, 55
Turbas, 107, 119
Twelve, The, 34, 36, 39

UNAG. *See* National Union of (Small) Farmers and Cattlemen
Underdevelopment, 58
Unemployment, 59, 81, 89
UNESCO. *See* United Nations Educational, Scientific, and Cultural Organization
UNICEF. *See* United Nations Children's Fund
Union of Nicaraguan Farmers (UPANIC), 46
Unions, 89, 102, 114
United Nations, 80, 132
United Nations Children's Fund (UNICEF), 90
United Nations Economic and Social Council (ECOSOC), 93
United Nations Educational, Scientific, and Cultural Organization (UNESCO), 97
United States, 62, 126. *See also* Central Intelligence Agency; Destabilization; Walker, William; *under* Honduras; Nicaragua; Sandinist Front of National Liberation; Somoza Debayle, Anastasio; Somoza García, Anastasio
University of California, 28
University of Maryland, 28

UPANIC. *See* Union of Nicaraguan
   Farmers
Upper class, 42, 56, 61, 84–85,
   87(fig.), 91
Uprisings (1978), 37, 41, 109, 130
Urbanization, 80–81
Urban workers, 41, 101, 102

Vaccination. *See* Inoculation
   campaigns
Vagrancy, 59
Vaho, 78
Vanderbilt, Cornelius, 58
Venezuela, 37, 48, 55, 140
Vigilancia revolucionaria, 109
Visión (news magazine), 66
Volcanos, 56
Voluntarism, 44, 45, 49, 70(illus.),
   90, 92, 93, 107, 109

Wages, 48, 89
Walker, William, 6, 14–15

War of Liberation (1978–1979), 43,
   61. *See also* Nicaragua,
   revolution
War of the Comuneros (1881), 15,
   59
Wells Fargo Bank, 64
Western lowlands, 2
West Germany, 133, 134
West Point Military Academy, 28
Wheelock, Jaime, 105(port.)
Whelan, Thomas, 128
Women, 42, 84, 107
Woodcarving, 77
Working class, 69, 91
World Bank, 46, 48, 69

Year of Literacy (1980), 96
Yugoslavia, 68

Zelaya, José Santos, 6, 15–18, 61,
   123, 124
Zelaya department, 82, 83
Zeledón, Benjamín, 6, 19–20, 124

DATE DUE	
NOV 30	
MAR 25 2003	